Jimmy Swaggart
100 Favorites

ISBN 978-1-934655-34-4
13-004 © 1981
JIMMY SWAGGART MINISTRIES
P.O. BOX 262550
Baton Rouge, Louisiana 70826-2550
Website: www.jsm.org • Email: info@jsm.org
(225) 768-7000
All rights reserved. Printed in the U.S.A.
Unauthorized reproductions is a violation of applicable laws.

(No part of this publication may be reproduced or transmitted in any form or by any means, electronic or mechanical, including photocopy, recording, or any other information storage and retrieval system, without permission in writing from the publisher.)

This songbook will add a new dimension to your spiritual life and development. God has used many of these songs in altar calls around the world in winning the lost to Jesus Christ. These song titles have been selected as part if a growing library of song treasures. These songs will spiritually enrich you soul and bless you abundantly over and over again. God bless you.

TITLE LIST

A SONG HOLY ANGELS CANNOT SING	46
AMAZING GRACE	151
BECAUSE HE LIVES	44
CITY OF GOLD	26
COME AND DINE	150
COME, HOLY SPIRIT	65
DADDY SANG BASS	146
DELIVERANCE WILL COME	112
FARTHER ALONG	154
GIVE THEM ALL TO JESUS	66
GO TELL IT ON THE MOUNTAIN	132
GOD'S WONDERFUL PEOPLE	68
GONE	82
GOODBYE WORLD, GOODBYE	136
HALLELUJAH SQUARE	73
HAVE FAITH IN GOD	127
HE DID IT ALL FOR ME	105
HE KEEPS ME SINGING	176
HE LIVES	138
HE SET ME FREE	96
HE TOUCHED ME	34
HE WAS THERE ALL THE TIME	130
HEARTMENDER	102
HEAVEN'S JUBILEE	32
HE'S GOT THE WHOLE WORLD IN HIS HANDS	113
HIS EYE IS ON THE SPARROW	12
HIS NAME IS WONDERFUL	14
HOLY SPIRIT, THOU ART WELCOME	155
I SEE JESUS	118
I JUST FEEL LIKE SOMETHING GOOD IS ABOUT TO HAPPEN	84
I SHOULD HAVE BEEN CRUCIFIED	174
I WILL SERVE THEE	133
I'D RATHER BE AN OLD TIME CHRISTIAN	128
IF THAT ISN'T LOVE	22
I'LL BE SATISFIED	87
I'LL MEET YOU IN THE MORNING	164
I'M GONNA MAKE IT THROUGH	5
I'M STANDING ON THE SOLID ROCK	18
IT'S OVER NOW	56
I'VE BEEN TO CALVARY	124
I'VE GOT CONFIDENCE	172
JESUS IS COMING SOON	144
JESUS WILL OUTSHINE THEM ALL	166
JOHN THE REVELATOR	148
JUST A CLOSER WALK WITH THEE	86
JUST A LITTLE TALK WITH JESUS	158
JUST ANY DAY NOW	116

KEEP ON THE FIRING LINE	92
KEEP WALKING	108
LEANING ON THE EVERLASTING ARMS	104
LEARNING TO LEAN	106
LEAVIN' ON MY MIND	40
LET'S JUST PRAISE THE LORD	90
LOOKING FOR A CITY	160
LOVE LIFTED ME	64
LOVE WILL ROLL THE CLOUDS AWAY	24
MANSION OVER THE HILLTOP	38
MY TRIBUTE	28
NEARER MY GOD, TO THEE	61
OH COME, ANGEL BAND	163
REACH OUT AND TOUCH THE LORD	54
REACH OUT TO JESUS	134
REDEMPTION DRAWETH NIGH	98
RISE AGAIN	36
ROOM AT THE CROSS	60
SET ANOTHER PLACE AT THE TABLE	20
SOMETHING BEAUTIFUL	30
SOMETIMES ALLELUIA	79
SOON AND VERY SOON	70
SPECIAL DELIVERY	50
SUPPERTIME	77
SWEET, SWEET SPIRIT	162
TEN THOUSAND YEARS	100
THAT GLAD REUNION DAY	15
THAT'S JUST LIKE JESUS	58
THAT'S THE MAN I'M LOOKING FOR	140
THE EASTERN GATE	88
THE GREAT REWARD	110
THE KING IS COMING	74
THE LIGHTHOUSE	122
THE UNCLOUDED DAY	72
THERE IS A RIVER	10
THERE'S SOMETHING ABOUT THAT NAME	62
THIS COULD BE THE DAWNING OF THAT DAY	168
THIS IS JUST WHAT HEAVEN MEANS TO ME	16
THROUGH IT ALL	48
TOURING THAT CITY	42
TURN TO JESUS	78
TURN YOUR RADIO ON	114
UNTIL YOU'VE KNOWN THE LOVE OF GOD	156
VICTORY IN JESUS	120
WAIT'LL YOU SEE MY BRAND NEW HOME	94
WASTED YEARS	52
WE'LL SOON BE DONE WITH TROUBLES AND TRIALS	152
WHAT SINS ARE YOU TALKING ABOUT	142
WHEN GOD DIPS HIS PEN OF LOVE IN MY HEART	170
WHEN I WAKE UP TO SLEEP NO MORE	80
WHEN THE SAINTS GO MARCHING IN	97
WHEN WE ALL GET TO HEAVEN	89
WILL THE CIRCLE BE UNBROKEN	126

I'm Gonna Make It Through

JAMES JOHNSON
Arr. by Bill Hedrick

1. When I wake up in the morn-ing and I start a brand new day, I have this hap-py feel-ing that ev-'ry-thing's gon-na be o-kay, 'Cause you see I have a help-

© Copyright 1979 by JIMMY SWAGGART MINISTRIES P.O. Box 2550, Baton Rouge, LA 70821
All Rights Reserved

-er Who's walk-in' right by my side, And my friend, His name is Je-sus, Yes, He's gon-na be my guide.

CHORUS

And I'm gon-na make it through, yes, I am:

Make it through, yes, I am, And I'll not be defeated, I'll sing a happy song; And I'm gonna make it through the day, 'Cause to Jesus I belong.

2. Now when you seem just a little un-hap-py And you seem just a lit-tle blue, ___ If you'll lis-ten I will tell ___ you The thing that you should do. ___ Just have a lit-tle talk with Je-sus and He'll take you by the hand, ___ He'll

drive your sor-rows all a-way, Yes, He's that kind of Man.

CODA

Yes, I'm gon-na make it through the day 'Cause to Je-sus I be-long.

There Is A River

Words and Music by
DAVID and MAX SAPP

1. There came a sound from Heav-en,— As a rush-ing, might-y wind,—
2. There was a thirst-y wo-man,— Who was draw-ing from a well,—

It filled their hearts with sing-ing,— And gave them peace with-in;—
Her life was ruined and wast-ed,— Her soul was bound for hell;—

The Proph-et gave this prom-ise,— "The Spir-it will de-scend,—
— Then she met the Mas-ter,— Who told of her great sin,—

And from your in-ner be-ing— A riv-er with no end."—
And if you drink this wa-ter,— You'll nev-er thirst a-gain.—

© Copyright 1969 by DAVID and MAX SAPP
All Rights Reserved.   Used by Permission.

CHORUS

There is a riv-er ___ that flows from deep with-in, ___
There is a riv-er ___ that flows from God a-bove, ___

There is a foun-tain ___ that frees the soul from sin. ___
There is a foun-tain ___ that's filled with His great love. ___

Come to this wa-ter, ___ There is a vast sup-ply, ___

There is a riv-er, ___ That nev-er ___ shall run dry! ___

His Eye Is On The Sparrow

Mrs C.D. MARTIN
CHAS. H. GABRIEL

1. Why should I feel dis-cour-aged, Why should the shad-ows come, Why should my heart be lone-ly, And long for heav'n and home, When Je-sus is my por-tion? My con-stant friend is He;
2. "Let not your heart be troub-led," His ten-der word I hear, And rest-ing on His good-ness, I lose my doubts and fears; Tho' by the path He lead-eth, But one step I may see;
3. When-ev-er I am tempt-ed, When-ev-er clouds a-rise, When song gives place to sigh-ing, When hope with-in me dies, I draw the clo-ser to Him, From care He sets me free;

This Arrangement © 1981 by JIMMY SWAGGART MINISTRIES, P.O. Box 2550, Baton Rouge, LA 70821

His eye is on the spar-row,— And I know He watch-es me;
His eye is on the spar-row,— And I know He watch-es me;
His eye is on the spar-row,— And I know He cares for me;

His eye is on the spar-row,— And I know He watch-es me.
His eye is on the spar-row,— And I know He watch-es me.
His eye is on the spar-row,— And I know He cares for me.

I sing be-cause I'm hap-py,⎯⎯ I sing be-cause I'm free,⎯⎯
 I'm hap-py, I'm free,

For His eye is on the spar-row,— And I know He watch-es me.—

His Name Is Wonderful

Words and Music by
AUDREY MIEIR

His name is Wonderful. His name is Wonderful, His name is Wonderful, Jesus, my Lord;___ He is the mighty King. Master of ev'rything, His name is Wonderful, Jesus, my Lord. He's the great Shepherd, the Rock of all ages, Almighty God is He;___ Bow down before Him, Love and adore Him, His name is Wonderful, Jesus, my Lord.

© Copyright 1959 by MANNA MUSIC, INC., 2111 Kenmere Ave., Burbank, CA. 91504
All Rights Reserved. International Copyright Secured. Used by Permission.

That Glad Reunion Day

Words and Music by
ADGER M. PACE

1. There will be a hap-py meet-ing in heav-en I know.
2. There with-in the ho-ly cit-y we'll sing and re-joice.
3. When we live a mil-lion years in that won-der-ful place.

When we see the man-y loved ones we've known here be-low,
Prais-ing Christ the bless-ed Sav-iour with heart and with voice.
Bask-ing in the love of Je-sus, be-hold-ing His face.

Gath-ered on the bless-ed hill-tops with hearts all a-glow,
Tell Him how we came to love Him and make Him our choice.
It will seem but just a mo-ment of prais-ing His grace,

D.S. There with all the ho-ly an-gels and loved ones to stay

That will be a glad re-un-ion day. Glad
That will be a glad re-un-ion day.

CHORUS

Glad day, a won-der-ful day. Glad day, a glo-ri-ous day;
That will be a hap-py day, yes a won-der-ful day. That will be a hap-py day, yes, a glo-ri-ous day;

© Copyright 1940, ADGER M. PACE, JAMES D. VAUGHAN, MUSIC PUBLISHER, owner.
Assn. to CHURCH OF GOD PUBLISHING HOUSE. All Rights Reserved. Used by Permission.

This Is Just What Heaven Means To Me

1. A country where no twilight shadows deepen,
   Unending day where night will never be;
   A city where the storm clouds cannot gather,
   Oh, this is just what Heaven means to me!

2. A place where there is no misunderstanding,
   And from all enmity and strife we're free;
   No unkind words to wound the heart are spoken,
   Now this is just what Heaven means to me!

3. And when at last we see the face of Jesus,
   Before whose image other loves all flee;
   And when they crown him Lord of all I'll be there,
   For this is just what Heaven means to me!

This Arrangement ©1981 by JIMMY SWAGGART MINISTRIES, P.O. Box 2550, Baton Rouge, LA 70821

What joy 'twill be when we get o-ver yon-der, And join the throng a-round the crys-tal sea! To meet our loved ones and crown Christ for-ev-er, Oh, this is just what Heav-en means to me!

I'm Standing On The Solid Rock

Words and Music by HAROLD LANE

1. Thru my dis-ap-point-ments, strife and dis-con-tent-ment, I cast my ev-'ry care on the Lord; No matter what ob-ses-sion, pain or deep de-pres-sion, I'm standing on the Solid Rock.

2. E-ven-tho He's gone now, I don't feel a-lone now, with comfort came the Spir-it of the Lord; Now with His word to guide me, from temp-ta-tions hide me, I'm standing on the Solid Rock.

3. Now I'm press-ing on-ward, each step leads me home-ward, I'm trust-ing in my Sav-ior day by day. And close is our re-la-tion, firm is its foun-da-tion, So on this Sol-id Rock I'll stay.

© Copyright 1977 by BEN L. SPEER.
All Rights Reserved and Controlled by BEN SPEER MUSIC, Box 40201, Nashville, 37204
International Copyright Secured.   Used by Permission.

CHORUS

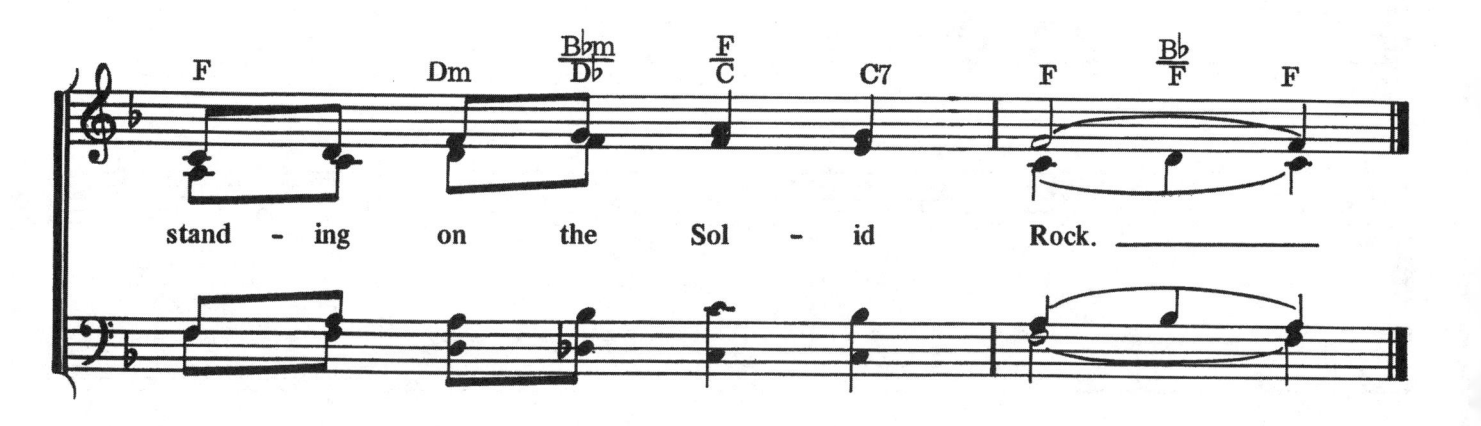

I'm stand-ing on the Rock of A-ges,
Stand-ing on the Rock, On the Rock of
Safe from all the storm that ra-ges,
Safe from ev-'ry storm, All the storm that
Rich but not from Sa-tan's wa-ges, I'm
Rich, in love I'm rich, Not from Sa-tan's
stand-ing on the Sol-id Rock.

Set Another Place At The Table

Words and Music by
AARON WILBURN
JOHN PRICE
and JOHN STALLS

1. In heav-en they've just re-ceived a res-er-va-tion, From a mis-sion-ar-y in a dis-tant land;— To ac-com-o-date a par-ty of be-liev-ers Who've just ac-cept-ed God's sal-va-tion plan.
2. Just as the an-gels say "all is read-y," God hears the cry from an-oth-er man;— And there has been an-oth-er birth in-to the king-dom And the head-wait-er hears one more com-mand.
3. If you have not an-swered your in-vi-ta-tion, It is en-graved for-ev-er in His hand;— And I've come to re-mind you of the hon-or To dine in the pre-sence of this man.

CHORUS
So, set an-oth-er place at the ta-ble and write an-oth-er name on the roll; Take

© Copyright 1979 by FIRST MONDAY MUSIC (a div. of WORD, INC.)
All Rights Reserved. International Copyright Secured. Used by Permission.

out an-oth-er robe, ___ shine up one more crown, an-oth-er child is heav-en bound! ___ Add an-oth-er verse to the cho-rus, ___ as the an-gels re-hearse ___ the wel-come song; ___ Set an-oth-er place at the ta-ble, ___ Soon the rest of the fam-'ly's com-in' home. ___

If That Isn't Love

Words and Music by
DOTTIE RAMBO

1. He left the splendor of Heaven Knowing His destiny Was the lonely hill of Golgotha, There to lay down His life for me.
2. Even in death He remembered The thief hanging by His side; He spoke with love and compassion, Then He took him to Paradise.

CHORUS

If that isn't love The ocean is dry;

© Copyright 1969 by HEARTWARMING MUSIC CO. (BMI).
International Copyright Secured. All Rights Reserved.
Printed by Permission of THE BENSON COMPANY, INC., Nashville.

There's no stars in the sky— And the spar-row— can't fly!— If that is-n't love— Then Heav-en's a myth,— There's no feel-ing like this— If that is-n't love.

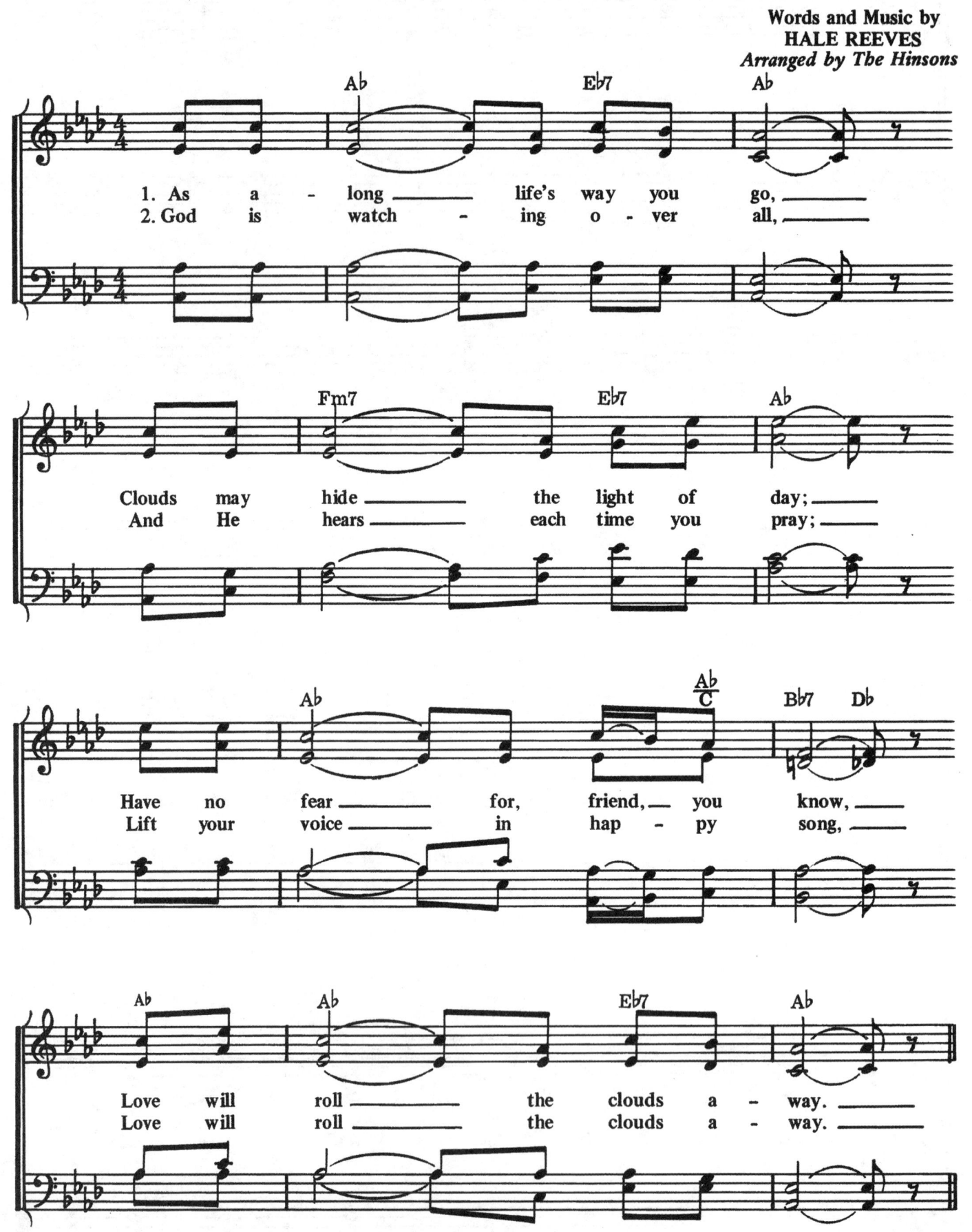

Love Will Roll The Clouds Away

Words and Music by
HALE REEVES
Arranged by The Hinsons

1. As a - long life's way you go,
2. God is watch - ing o - ver all,

Clouds may hide the light of day;
And He hears each time you pray;

Have no fear for, friend, you know,
Lift your voice in hap - py song,

Love will roll the clouds a - way.
Love will roll the clouds a - way.

© Copyright 1946 by THE STAMPS QUARTET MUSIC COMPANY, INC.
Copyright Renewed 1974. All Rights Reserved.

CHORUS

Love will roll _____ the clouds a-way, _____
Love will roll

Turn the dark - ness in - to day; _____
Turn the dark-ness in-to day; _____

I'm so glad _____ I now can say, _____
I'm so glad

Love will roll _____ the clouds a - way. _____
Love will roll

City Of Gold

Words and Music by
SHIRLEY COHRON

1. There's a cit-y that looks o'er the val-ley of death, And its glo-ry has nev-er been told; ___ Where the Lamb is the light ___ in the midst ___ of the night In that beau-ti-ful cit-y of gold. ___

2. There will be no more sor-row, pain, sick-ness or death, And the saints, they will nev-er grow old; ___ How I long for that cit-y where there nev-er comes a night In that beau-ti-ful cit-y of gold. ___

CHORUS

Where the

© Copyright 1970 by DIMENSION MUSIC (SESAC).
International Copyright Secured. All Rights Reserved.
Printed by Permission of THE BENSON COMPANY, INC., Nashville.

sun ___ nev-er sets, ___ And the leaves ___ nev-er fade; ___ And the right-eous for-ev-er will shine like the stars, In that beau-ti-ful cit-y of gold. ___ gold. ___

My Tribute
(TO GOD BE THE GLORY)

Words and Music by
ANDRAE CROUCH

How can I say thanks for the things You have done for me? Things so un-de-served, yet You give to prove Your love for me. The voic-es of a mil-lion an-gels could not ex-press my grat-i-tude; All that I am and ev-er hope to be I owe it all to Thee. To God be the glo-ry, to God, be the glo-ry, to God, be the
Blood He has saved me, with His pow'r, He has raised me, to God, be the

© Copyright 1971 by LEXICON MUSIC, INC. ASCAP
All Rights Reserved. International Copyright Secured. Used by Special Permission.

glo - ry for the things He has done. With His glo - ry for the things He has

done. Just let me live my life ___ let it be pleas - ing ___ Lord to

Thee; ___ And should I gain an - y praise, let it go to Cal - va - ry. With His

blood He has saved me, with His pow'r He has raised me, To

God ___ be the glo - ry for the things He has done. ___

Something Beautiful

GLORIA GAITHER CHORUS WILLIAM J. GAITHER

Some-thing beau-ti-ful, Some-thing good; All my con-fu-sion — He un-der-stood; All I had to of-fer Him — was bro-ken-ness and strife, — But He made some-thing — beau-ti-ful — of my life.

VERSE

If there ev-er were dreams that were loft-y and

© Copyright 1971 by WILLIAM J. GAITHER (ASCAP).
International Copyright Secured. All Rights Reserved.
Printed by Permission of THE BENSON COMPANY, INC., Nashville.

no-ble, they were my dreams at the start;— And the hopes for life's best were the hopes that I har-bored down deep in my heart; But my dreams turned to ash-es, my cas-tles all crum-bled, my for-tune turned to loss, So I wrapped it all in the rags of my life, and laid it at the cross! life!

Heaven's Jubilee

ADGER M. PACE G.T. SPEER

1. Some glad morn-ing we shall see — Je-sus in the air,
2. Seems that now I al-most see — all the saint-ed dead,
3. When with all that heav'n-ly host — we be-gin to sing,

Com-ing aft-er you and me, — joy is ours to share;
Ris-ing for that ju-bi-lee, — that is just a head;
Sing-ing in the Ho-ly Ghost, — how the heav'ns will ring;

What re-joic-ing there will be — when the saints shall rise,
In the twink-ling of an eye, — changed with them to be,
Mil-lions there will join the song, — with them we shall be

Head-ed for that ju-bi-lee, — yon-der in the skies.
All the liv-ing saints to fly — to that ju-bi-lee.
Prais-ing Christ thru a-ges long, — heav-en's ju-bi-lee.

This Arrangement © 1981 by JIMMY SWAGGART MINISTRIES, P.O.Box 2550, Baton Rouge, LA 70821

CHORUS

O, — what — sing - ing, O, — what — shout - ing,
What a day of sing - ing, sing - ing, what a day of shout - ing, shout - ing.

On that hap - py morn - ing when we all shall rise;
when we all shall glad - ly rise.

O, — what — glo - ry, Hal - le - lu - jah!
What a day of glo - ry, glo - ry, Glo - ry hal - le - lu - jah! Glo - ry!

When we meet our bless - ed Sav - ior in the skies.
Sav - ior yon - der in the skies.

He Touched Me

**Words and Music by
WILLIAM J. GAITHER**

Shack - led by a heav - y bur - den
Since I met this bless - ed Sav - ior,
'neath a load of guilt and shame,
since He cleansed and made me whole,
Then the hand of Je - sus touched me and
I will nev - er cease to praise Him I'll
now I am no long - er the same.
shout it while e - ter - ni - ty rolls.

© Copyright 1963 by WILLIAM J. GAITHER (ASCAP).
International Copyright Secured.   All Rights Reserved.
Printed by Permission of THE BENSON COMPANY, INC., Nashville.

CHORUS

He touched me, oh He touched me, And oh the joy that floods my soul, Something happened, and now I know He touched me and made me whole.

Rise Again

Words and Music by DALLAS HOLM

1. Go a-head, Drive the nails in my hands; Laugh at me where you stand; Go a-head, and say it isn't me; The day will come when you will see! 'Cause I'll (1,2) rise a-
2. Go a-head, and mock my name; My love for you is still the same; Go a-head, and bur-ry me; But ver-y soon I will be free! 'Cause I'll (3) come a-
3. Go a-head, and say I'm dead and gone, But you will see that you were wrong; Go a-head, and try to hide the Son; But all will see that I'm the One! 'Cause I'll

CHORUS

© Copyright 1977 by DIMENSION MUSIC (SESAC)
International Copyright Secured. All Rights Reserved.
Printed by Permission of THE BENSON COMPANY, INC., Nashville.

gain; Ain't no pow'r on earth can tie me down;
gain; Ain't no pow'r on earth can keep me back;

Yes, I'll rise a - gain,
Yes, I'll come a - gain,

1st & 2nd time D.C.
3rd time to Coda

Death can't keep me in the ground!
Come to take my peo - ple back!

CODA

Come to take my peo - ple back.

Mansion Over The Hilltop

Words and Music by
IRA F. STANPHILL

1. I'm satisfied with just a cottage below, A little silver and a little gold; But in that city where the ransomed will shine, I want a gold one that's silver-lined.
2. Tho often tempted, tormented and tested, And, like the prophet, my pillow a stone, And tho I find here no permanent dwelling, I know He'll give me a mansion my own.
3. Don't think me poor or deserted or lonely, I'm not discouraged, I'm heaven bound; I'm just a pilgrim in search of a city, I want a mansion, a harp and a crown.

© Copyright 1949. Renewal 1977 by IRA STANPHILL. Assn. to SINGSPIRATION,
Division of THE ZONDERVAN CORPORATION.
All Rights Reserved. Used by Permission.

CHORUS

I've got a mansion just over the hilltop, In that bright land where we'll never grow old; And some day yonder we will nevermore wander, But walk the streets that are purest gold.

Leavin' On My Mind

Words and Music by
RUSTY GOODMAN

1. The old house I'm living in is needing repair; The windows and the shutters are letting in the cold air; I say to myself, "I'm gonna fix 'em when I can get the time; But all I've been getting

2. So, I guess I should be looking for a better place to live; But I can't seem to get excited about the world and what it can give; I couldn't care less if I could buy it all with a solitary dime; For what good would a

©Copyright 1979 by FIRST MONDAY MUSIC (a div. of WORD, INC.)
All Rights Reserved. International Copyright Secured. Used by Permission.

late - ly   is leav - in' on ____ my mind. ____
world do me ___ with leav - in' on ____ my mind. ____

CHORUS
Late - ly all I got is leav - in' on ____ my mind; ____

Seems that's all I'm think - in' 'bout most of the time; But

soon and ver - y soon I'll leave ____ my trou - ble ____ far be - hind;

Late - ly I've got leav - in', leav - in' on ____ my mind. ____

Touring That City

Words and Music by
HAROLD LANE

1. Man-y times I have won-dered 'bout the sights of that cit-y, and
2. Here on earth we have trou-bles that to us seem so heav-y, but in

all that my eyes shall be-hold; I will see all the won-ders when I
Heav-en no one will be sad; Mom and Dad will be sing-ing, Heav-en's

en-ter that cit-y, there for-ev-er to be safe in His fold.
praise will be ring-ing for the dear-est Friend I ev-er had.

CHORUS

Some morn-ing you'll find me tour-ing that cit-y, where the Son of God is the

© Copyright 1973 by BEN SPEER MUSIC.
All Rights Reserved and Controlled by BEN SPEER MUSIC, Box 40201, Nashville 37204
International Copyright Secured.   Used by Permission.

Light,____ You'll find me there on the streets so pret-ty, made of gold,____ so pure and so bright;____ With Je-sus, the One, Who gave me the vic-t'ry, Who____ led me a-cross the di-vide,____ Some morn-ing you'll find me tour-ing that cit-y, where with Him I will ev-er a-bide.____

Because He Lives

Words by WILLIAM J. and GLORIA GAITHER

Music by WILLIAM J. GAITHER

1. God sent His son, They called Him Jesus,
2. How sweet to hold our new-born baby,
3. And then one day I'll cross that river,

He came to love, heal and for-give;
And feel the pride and joy He gives;
I'll fight life's fi - nal war with pain;

He lived and died to buy my par-don,
But great-er still the calm as-sur-ance,
And then as death gives way to vic-t'ry,

An emp-ty grave is there to prove my Sav-ior lives.
This child can face un-cer-tain days be-cause He lives.
I'll see the lights of glo-ry and I'll know He reigns.

© Copyright 1971 by WILLIAM J. GAITHER (ASCAP).
International Copyright Secured. All Rights Reserved.
Printed by Permission of THE BENSON COMPANY, INC., Nashville.

CHORUS

Be-cause He lives ___ I can face to-mor-row, ___
Be-cause He lives ___ all fear is gone; ___
Be-cause I know ___ He holds the fu-ture, ___
And life is worth the liv-ing, just be-cause He lives. ___

A Song Holy Angels Cannot Sing

Words and Music by
GORDON JENSEN

1. An-gels nev-er knew the joy that is mine,
For the blood has nev-er washed their sins a-way;
Tho' they sing in Heav-en there will come a time
When si-lent-ly they'll lis-ten to me sing "A-maz-ing Grace."

2. "Ho-ly is the Lord," the an-gels sing,
Be-fore the throne of God con-tin-ual-ly;
For me to join their song will be a nat-'ral thing,
But they just won't know the words to "Love Lift-ed Me."

© Copyright 1973 by JENSEN MUSIC (ASCAP).
International Copyright Secured. All Rights Reserved.
Printed by Permission of THE BENSON COMPANY, INC., Nashville.

47

CHORUS

And it's a song holy angels cannot sing, "Amazing Grace, How sweet the sound!" It's a song holy angels cannot sing, "I once was lost, but now I'm found."

Through It All

Words and Music by ANDRAE CROUCH

1. I've had many tears and sorrows, I've had questions for tomorrow, There've been times I didn't know right from wrong; But in ev'ry situation God gave blessed consolation That my trials come to

2. I've been to lots of places, And I've seen a lot of faces, There've been times I felt so all alone But in my lonely hours, Yes, those precious lonely hours, Jesus let me know that

3. I thank God for the mountains, And I thank Him for the valleys, I thank Him for the storms He bro't me thru For if I never had a problem I wouldn't know that He could solve them, I'd never know what

© Copyright 1971 by MANNA MUSIC, INC., 2111 Kenmere Ave., Burbank, CA. 91504
International Copyright Secured. All Rights Reserved. Used by Permission.

CHORUS

on-ly make me strong.
I was His own. Thru it all, _____
faith in God could do.

Thru it all, _____ (O,) I've learned to trust in Jesus, I've

learned to trust in God; Thru it all, _____ Thru it all, _____

_____ I've learned to depend upon His Word. _____

Special Delivery

Words and Music by
RON and CAROL HARRIS

1. Nev-er was an-y-one like Him, nev-er will one be the same. Ti-ny babe, in-fant King, Sav-ior, we wor-ship and hon-or the pow'r of His name. Oh, He came
2. Where He went love was there al-so, where He was love showed the way. Those who saw knew He was ho-ly, and I see what they saw to this ver-y day. Oh, He came spe-cial de-liv-er-y, wrapped up in love,
3. When I'm called I will go glad-ly, I will not grieve for the past, for I know where I'll be go-ing. And I will be go-ing to see Him at last. I'm go-ing

bound by a prom-ise, sealed by a dove; and filled with the
Spir-it, car-ried by grace, you knew where He was go-ing — by the
Spir-it, car-ried by grace, you'll know where I am go-ing — by the

Last time to Coda

look on His face. 3. And
look on my face. I'm go-ing

D.S. al Coda

CODA

look on my face.

Wasted Years

Words and Music by
WALLY FOWLER

Medium tempo, with feeling

1. Have you wan-dered a-long on life's path-way,
2. Search for wis-dom and seek un-der-stand-ing,
3. Don't you know Je-sus died for all sin-ners.

Have you lived with-out love, a life of tears;
There is Some-one who knows, and al-ways hears;
He loves you and your guilt He glad-ly bears;

Have you searched for the great hid-den mean-ing,
Give it up! Give it up! the load you're bear-ing,
Come to Him! Come to Him! your sin con-fess-ing

or is your life filled with long wast-ed years?
you can't go on in a life of wast-ed years.
you can go on with a life of fruit-ful years.

© Copyright 1959 by GOSPELTONE MUSIC PUBLICATIONS, P.O.Box 15826, Baton Rouge, LA 70895
All Rights Reserved. International Copyright Secured. Used by Permission.

CHORUS

Wast-ed years, wast-ed years, Oh, how fool-ish, as you walk on in dark-ness and fears; Turn a-round, turn a-round, God is call-ing, He's call-ing you from a life of wast-ed years.

Reach Out And Touch The Lord

BILL HARMON

If your heart is sad and lone-ly — There's no joy an-y-where. There is no one — left to com-fort — There's no one left that seems to care. O just cast your cares on Je-sus — and on those strong arms — just re-lax. O reach out and touch my Lord — as —

© Copyright 1981 by BILL HARMON. All Rights Reserved.

He goes by. Reach out and touch the Lord as He goes by. You will find He's not too busy just to hear your heart's cry. He's passing by this very moment, your needs He'll supply. Reach out and touch the Lord as He goes by.

It's Over Now

**Words and Music by
RUSTY GOODMAN**

CHORUS

It's o-ver now, It's o-ver, I'm go-ing home. It's o-ver now, It can't be long. The pri-sons of my past could-n't hold me, I'm free at last. My Fa-ther I see, His arms reach-ing for me; It's o-ver now

last time to Coda

© Copyright 1979 by FIRST MONDAY MUSIC (a div. Of WORD, INC.)
All Rights Reserved. Used by Permission.

1. When I look back to yesterday and upon the many years I wasted, And I think about the many nights of hunger that I spent out in the cold. I remember warming by the fire at father's house, the food and how it tasted. And knowin' that the life I'm leading is needin' love, and love's at home. It's over

2. I can hear my Father sayin', "Go, kill the fatted calf and spread the table; Then go and tell the singers to prepare, to sing the welcome song. Then bring the finest ring of gold and with it, bring the finest robe of sable, To place upon the cold and weary shoulders of my child that's coming home."

now.

That's Just Like Jesus

Words and Music by
GARLAND CRAFT

1. When you are lone - ly, and bro - ken - heart - ed;
2. When you a - buse Him, He's bro - ken - heart - ed;

Je - sus will help you, He is your
yet He still loves us, He an - swers our

friend; And all of your prob -
prayers; We should be thank -

lems, He will re - move them, and leave you
ful He is for - giv - ing, and leave for His

©Copyright 1974 by SILVERLINE MUSIC, INC. (BMI)
329 Rockland Road, Hendersonville, TN 37075
All Rights Reserved. International Copyright Secured.

smil - ing, so full of joy.
dy - ing, we can be free.

CHORUS

That's just like Je - sus, that's just like Je - sus; nev - er far, al - ways near; that's just like Je - sus.

Room At The Cross

Words and Music by
IRA F. STANPHILL

1. The cross up-on which Je-sus died — Is a shel-ter in which we can hide, — And its grace so free is suf-fi-cient for me, And deep is its foun-tain, as wide as the sea.
2. Tho' mil-lions have found Him a friend, — And have turned from the sins they have sinned, — The Sav-ior still waits to o-pen the gate, And wel-come a sin-ner be-fore it's too late.
3. The hand of my Sav-ior is strong, — And the love of my Sav-ior is long; — Through sun-shine or rain, through loss or in gain, The blood flows from Cal-v'ry to cleanse ev-'ry stain.

CHORUS

There's room at the cross for you, — There's room at the cross for you; — Though mil-lions have come, There's

©Copyright 1946. Renewal 1974 by IRA STANPHILL. Assn. to SINGSPIRATION, div. of THE ZONDERVAN CORP.
All Rights Reserved. Used by Permission

still room for one, Yes, there's room at the cross for you.

Nearer My God, To Thee

SARAH F. ADAMS
LOWELL MASON

1. Near - er, my God to Thee, Near - er to Thee;
2. Tho' like a wan - der - er, The sun goes down;
3. There let the way ap - pear, Steps un - to heav'n;

E'en tho' it be a cross That rais - eth me.
Dark - ness be o - ver me, My rest a stone.
All that Thou send - est me, In mer - cy giv'n.

D.S. Near - er my God to Thee, Near - er to Thee.

Still all my song shall be, Near - er, my God, to Thee.
Yet in my dreams I'd be, Near - er, my God, to Thee.
An - gels to beck - on me Near - er, my God, to Thee.

This Arrangement © 1981 by JIMMY SWAGGART MINISTRIES, P.O.Box 2550, Baton Rouge, LA 70821

There's Something About That Name

Words by
WILLIAM J. and GLORIA GAITHER

Music by
WILLIAM J. GAITHER

Je - sus, Je - sus, Je - sus there's just some - thing a - bout that name.

Mas - ter, Sav - ior, Je - sus, like the fra - grance af - ter the rain.

© Copyright 1970 by WILLIAM J. GAITHER (ASCAP).
International Copyright Secured. All Rights Reserved.
Printed by Permission of THE BENSON COMPANY, INC., Nashville.

Je - sus Je - sus, Je - sus let all heav - en and earth pro - claim. Kings and king - doms will all pass a - way but there's some - thing a - bout that name.

Love Lifted Me

JAMES ROWE
HOWARD E. SMITH

1. I was sinking deep in sin, Far from the peaceful shore,— Very deeply stained within, Sinking to rise no more;— But the Master of the sea Heard my despairing cry,— From the waters lifted me; Now safe am I.
2. All my heart to Him I give, Ever to Him I'll cling,— In His blessed presence live, Ever His praises sing;— Love so mighty and so true Merits my soul's best songs;— Faithful, loving service, too To Him belongs.
3. Souls in danger, look above, Jesus completely saves,— He will lift you by His love Out of the angry waves;— He's the Master of the sea, Billows His will obey; He your Saviour wants to be, Be saved today.

CHORUS

Love lifted me! (even me!) Love lifted me! (even me!) When nothing else could help, Love lifted me. Love lifted me.

© Copyright 1912 by JOHN T. BENSON, Jr. Renewed 1940. Copyright extended.
All Rights Reserved. International Copyright Secured. Used by Permission.

Come, Holy Spirit

Words by WILLIAM J.
and GLORIA GAITHER

Music by
WILLIAM J. GAITHER

1. Come, as a wis-dom to chil-dren, Come, as new sight to the blind, Come, Lord, as strength to my weak-ness; Take me: soul, bod-y and mind.
2. Come, as a rest to the wea-ry, Come, as a balm for the sore, Come, as a dew to my dry-ness: Fill me with joy, ev-er-more,
3. Come, like a spring in the des-ert, Come, to the with-ered of soul; Oh, let Thy sweet heal-ing pow-er, Touch me, and make me whole.

Come, Ho-ly Spir-it, I need Thee, Come, sweet Spir-it, I pray; Come, in Thy strength and Thy pow-er, Come, in Thy own gen-tle way.

Coda sing after last chorus only - ad lib

Come, in Thy own, gen-tle way.

© Copyright 1964 by WILLIAM J. GAITHER (ASCAP).
All Rights Reserved. International Copyright Secured.
Printed by Permission of THE BENSON COMPANY, INC., Nashville.

Give Them All To Jesus

Words and Music by
PHIL JOHNSON

Are you tired of chas-in' pre-ty rain-bows,
And are you tired of spin-in' round and round?
Wrap up all the shat-tered dreams of your life
And at the feet of Je-sus lay them down.

He nev-er said you'd on-ly see sun-shine,
And He nev-er said there'd be no rain,
He on-ly prom-ised a heart full of sing-ing
A-bout the ver-y things that once brought pain.

© Copyright 1975 by DIMENSION MUSIC (SESAC).
International Copyright Secured. All Rights Reserved.
Printed by Permission of THE BENSON COMPANY, INC., Nashville

CHORUS

Give them all, give them all, give them all to Je-sus. Shattered dreams, wounded hearts and broken toys; Give them all, give them all, give them all to Je-sus. And He will turn your sorrow into joy.

God's Wonderful People

Words and Music by
LANNY WOLFE

I love the thrill that I feel when I get to-geth-er with God's won-der-ful peo-ple,— Love the thrill that I feel when I get to-geth-er with God's won-der-ful peo-ple;— What a sight just to see all the hap-py fa-ces,— prais-ing God in heav-en-ly pla-ces; What a thrill that I feel when I get to-geth-er with

© Copyright 1974 by LANNY WOLFE MUSIC CO. (SESAC).
International Copyright Secured. All Rights Reserved.
Printed by Permission of THE BENSON COMPANY, INC., Nashville.

God's _____ won-der-ful peo - ple. _____

1. O what joy His love af-fords when we meet in one ac-cord,
2. It can be just an-y-where, two or three are gath-ered there,
3. On that great re-un-ion day when our Lord says, "Come a-way,"

And we lift our hearts in praise un-to the Lord;
That the Spir-it of the Lord will be there, too;
And the saints from ev-'ry land sweep thru the gates;

There's no place I'd rather be than with the ones who've been set
There's no fel-low-ship so sweet, there's no thrill that can com-
Join-ing loved ones 'round the throne, at last we'll all be gath-ered

free, I'm so glad I'm in God's great big fam-i-ly.
pete With the thrill I feel when-ev-er God's chil-dren meet. I love the
home, That will be the great-est thrill we've ev-er known.

Soon And Very Soon

Words and Music by
ANDRAE CROUCH

1. Soon and ver-y soon — we are goin' to see the King,
2. No more cry-in' there — we are goin' to see the King,
3. No more dy-in' there — we are goin' to see the King,
4. Soon and ver-y soon — we are goin' to see the King,

Soon and ver-y soon — we are goin' to see the King,
No more cry-in' there — we are goin' to see the King,
No more dy-in' there — we are goin' to see the King,
Soon and ver-y soon — we are goin' to see the King,

Soon and ver-y soon — we are goin' to see the King,
No more cry-in' there — we are goin' to see the King,
No more dy-in' there — we are goin' to see the King,
Soon and ver-y soon — we are goin' to see the King,

© Copyright 1976 by LEXICON MUSIC, INC. / CROUCH MUSIC
All Rights Reserved. International Copyright Secured. Used by Special Permission.

Hal - le - lu - jah, ___ Hal - le - lu - jah, ___ we're goin' to see the King! ___ Hal - le - lu - jah, Hal - le - lu - jah, Hal - le - lu - jah, Hal - le - lu - jah.

The Uncloudy Day

Words and Music by
J.K. ALWOOD

1. O they tell me of a home far be-yond the sky, O they tell me of a home ____ far a-way; Yes, they tell me of a home where no storms ev-er rise, O they tell me of an un-cloud-ed day.
2. O they tell me of a home where my friends have gone, O they tell me of a land ____ far a-way; O they tell me of a home in e-ter-nal bloom, O they tell me of a love-ly ____ land.
3. O they tell me that He smiles on His chil-dren there, And His smile ____ drives ____ sor-rows all a-way; And they tell me that no heart-aches shall ev-er come, O that love-ly land of un-cloud-ed day.

CHORUS

O that land of cloud-less day, O that land of ____ un-cloud-ed sky.

This Arrangement © 1981 by JIMMY SWAGGART MINISTRIES, P.O. Box 2550, Baton Rouge, LA 70821

Hallelujah Square

**Words and Music by
RAY OVERHOLT**

1. I saw a blind man, tap-ping a-long, Los-ing his way as he passed thru the throng; Tears filled my eyes, I said, "Friend, you can't see", With a smile on his face, he re-plied to me.
2. Now I saw a crip-ple, drag-ging his feet, He could-n't walk like we do down the street; I said, "My friend, I feel sor-ry for you", But he said, "Up in heav-en I'm gonna walk just like you."
3. Now I saw an old man, gasp-ing for breath, Soon he'd be gone as his eyes closed in death; He looked at me, said, "Boy, don't look so blue, I'm going up to heav-en, how a-bout you?"

CHORUS
I'll see all my friends in Hal-le-lu-jah Square, What a won-der-ful time we'll all have up there; We'll sing and praise Je-sus, His glo-ry to share, {And you'll not see one blind man / And you'll not see one crip-ple / And we'll all live for-ev-er} in Hal-le-lu-jah Square.

© Copyright 1969 by RAY OVERHOLT MUSIC. Arr. © 1974 by RAY OVERHOLT MUSIC.
All Rights Reserved. Used by Permission.

The King Is Coming

Words by
WILLIAM J. and GLORIA GAITHER and CHARLES MILHUFF

Music by
WILLIAM J. GAITHER

The mar-ket place is emp-ty, no more traf-fic in the streets, all the build-ers tools are si-lent, no more time to har-vest wheat; bus-y house-wives cease their la-bors, in the court-room no de-bate, work on earth is all sus-pend-ed as the King comes thro' the gate. Hap-py fa-ces line the hall-ways, those whose lives have been re-deemed, bro-ken

© Copyright 1970 by WILLIAM J. GAITHER (ASCAP).
International Copyright Secured. All Rights Reserved.
Printed by Permission of THE BENSON COMPANY, INC., Nashville.

homes that He has mend-ed, those from pris-on He has freed; Lit-tle chil-dren and the a-ged hand in hand stand all a-glow, who were crip-pled, bro-ken, ru-ined, clad in gar-ments white as snow. I can hear the char-iots rum-ble, I can see the march-ing throng. The flur-ry of God's trum-pets spell the end of sin and wrong; Re-gal robes are now un-fold-ing, heav-en's grand-stands all in place, heav-en's choir is now as-sem-bled, start to sing A-maz-ing Grace! Oh, the

REFRAIN

King is com-ing! The King is com-ing! I just heard the trum-pet sound-ing and now His face I see, oh, the King is com-ing! The King is com-ing! Praise God, He's com-ing for me. Oh, the me.

Supper Time

Words and Music by
IRA F. STANPHILL

1. Many years ago in days of childhood, I used to play till evening shadows come; Then, winding down an old familiar pathway, I heard my mother call at set of sun.
2. One day beside her bedside I was kneeling, And angel wings were winnowing the air; She heard the call for suppertime in heaven, And now I know she's waiting for me there.
3. In visions now I see her standing yonder, And her familiar voice I hear once more; The banquet table's ready up in heaven, It's suppertime upon the golden shore.

CHORUS

Come home, come home, it's supper time! The shadows lengthen fast; _____ time! We're going home at last. _____

© Copyright 1950. Renewal 1978 by IRA STANPHILL. Assn. to SINGSPIRATION, Div. of THE ZONDERVAN CORP.
All Rights Reserved.   Used by Permission.

Turn To Jesus

Words and Music by
HAL and RACHEL NEWMAN

1. Why in the world won't the world turn to Jesus? Why won't the world get together ____ and pray? Now is the time if we ever did need Him.
2. What will we do when the night is approaching? Where will we go to find shelter from the storm? Only to Him who is waiting to hold us

Jesus is the power, Jesus is the way.
high above the water, safe within His arms.

CHORUS
Turn to Jesus, turn to Jesus ____ He's the One you'd better work for on the street. You can stand up on the promises He made you ____ 'cause He never made a promise He can't keep.

© Copyright 1981 by PRIME TIME MUSIC, a div. of J. AARON BROWN & ASSOC., INC.
All Rights Reserved. International Copyright Secured.

Sometimes Alleluia

Words and Music by
CHUCK GIRARD

CHORUS

Some-times Al-le-lu-ia, some-times praise the Lord. Some-times gent-ly sing-ing, Our hearts in one ac-cord.

VERSE

Oh, let us lift our voic-es. Look to-ward the sky and start to sing. Oh, let us now re-turn His love. Just let our voic-es ring. Oh, let us feel His pres-ence. Let the sound of prais-es fill the air. Oh, let us sing the song of Je-sus love to peo-ple ev-'ry-where.

Oh, let our joy be un-con-fined. Let us sing with free-dom un-re-strained. Let's take this feel-ing that we feel now Out-side these walls and let it ring. Oh, let the spir-it o-ver-flow. As we are filled from head to toe. We love you Fa-ther, Son and Ho-ly Ghost, and we want this world to know.

© 1974 by DUNAMIS MUSIC, 8319 Lankershim Blvd., North Hollywood, CA 91605.
All Rights Reserved. Used by Permission.

When I Wake Up To Sleep No More

Words and Music by
MARION W. EASTERLING

1. What a glad tho't some won-der-ful morn-ing, I shall hear Ga-briel's trum-pet sound, when I wake up to sleep no more; Ris-ing to meet my bless-ed Re-deem-er, with a glad shout, I'll leave the ground, when I wake up to sleep no more.

2. Glo-ry to God, I'll have a new bod-y, changed in the twink-ling of an eye, when I wake up to sleep no more; Leav-ing be-hind all trou-ble and sor-row, bound for that cit-y up-on high, when I wake up to sleep no more.

3. I shall be-hold the beau-ties of Heav-en with the re-deemed of ev-'ry race, 'Neath the green trees be-side the still wa-ters I shall then find a rest-ing place, when I wake up to sleep no more.

CHORUS

On some glad morn-ing, jew-els a-dorn-ing, When I wake up to sleep no more, Hap-py I'll

© Copyright 1944 by STAMPS-BAXTER MUSIC & PTG. CO. in "Zion's Call".
© Renewed 1972. All Rights Reserved. Used by Permission.

O - ver in glo - ry tell - ing the sto - ry; With the re -
be on heav - en's bright shore;

deemed of all the a - ges prais - ing the One whom I a - dore, when I wake

up _____ When I wake up _____ to sleep no more. _____ to sleep no more.

CODA

When I wake up Some hap - py day, love I'll fly a - way, when I wake
 on wings of

up _____ When I wake up _____ to sleep no more. _____ to sleep no more.

Gone

Words and Music by ELDRIDGE FOX

1. Mar-y came un-to the tomb of Je-sus, The stone was moved and He had gone a-way; The an-gel said, "Fear not, I know whom seek ye, But He is ris-en," This she heard Him say.

2. My friend, if you don't know my ris-en Sav-iour, I beg of you, don't wait too late to pray; Don't wait un-til His bride has been com-plet-ed, Don't wait un-til you hear Him say, "It's too late."

© Copyright 1974 by KINGSMEN PUBLISHING CO. (BMI).
International Copyright Secured. All Rights Reserved.
Printed by Permission of THE BENTON COMPANY, INC., Nashville.

CHORUS

Gone, the stone is rolled back, Gone, the tomb is empty,

Gone, to sit at the Father's side;

Gone, over death triumphant, Gone, sin is defeated,

Gone, He lives forevermore.

I Just Feel Like Something Good Is About To Happen

Words and Music by
WILLIAM J. GAITHER

1. I just feel like some-thing good is a-bout to hap-pen,
2. I have learned in all that hap-pens— just to praise Him,
3. Yes, I've no-ticed all the bad news— in the pa-per,

I just feel like some-thing good is on— its way;
For I know He's work-ing all things for— my good;
And it seems like things are bleak-er ev-'ry day;

He has prom-ised that He'd o-pen all of Heav-en,
Ev-'ry tear I shed is worth all the in-vest-ment,
But for this child of God it makes no dif-f'rence,

— And broth-er, it— could hap-pen an-y day.
For I know He'll see— me through, He said He would.
Be-cause it's bound to get bet-ter eith-er way.

© Copyright 1974 by WILLIAM J. GAITHER (ASCAP).
International Copyright Secured. All Rights Reserved.
Printed by Permission of THE BENSON COMPANY, INC., Nashville.

When God's people humble themselves to call on Jesus,
He has promised eye nor ear can hardly fathom,
I've never been more thrilled about tomorrow,

And they look to Heaven expecting as they pray;
All the things He has in store for those who pray;
Sunshine's always bursting through the skies of gray;

I just feel like something good is about to happen, And brother, this could be the very day.

Just A Closer Walk With Thee

ANONYMOUS

1. I am weak but Thou art strong, Je-sus keep me from all wrong.
2. Thru this world of toil and snares, If I fal-ter, Lord, who cares?
3. When my fee-ble life is o'er, Time for me will be no more;

I'll be sat-is-fied as long as I walk, let me walk close to Thee.
Who with me my bur-den shares none but Thee, dear Lord, none but Thee.
Guide me gent-ly, safe-ly o'er to Thy king-dom shore, to Thy shore.

Just a clos-er walk with Thee, Grant it, Je-sus, is my plea.

Dai-ly walk-ing close to Thee, Let it be, dear Lord, let it be.

This Arrangement © 1981 by JIMMY SWAGGART MINISTRIES, P.O. Box 2550, Baton Rouge, LA 70821

I'll Be Satisfied

Arr. by Lura Harris

1. When my soul is singing in the promise land above, I'll be satisfied. Praising Christ the Savior for redeeming grace and love.
2. When I meet the ransomed over on the golden shore, I'll be satisfied. There I'll join the angels singing praise forevermore.

CHORUS

I'll be satisfied. I'll be satisfied. I'll be satisfied. When my soul is resting in the presence of the Lord, I'll be satisfied.

This Arrangement © 1981 by JIMMY SWAGGART MINISTRIES, P.O. Box 2550, Baton Rouge, LA 70821

The Eastern Gate

I. G. MARTIN — Arr. by I. G. MARTIN

1. I will meet you in the morning, Just inside the Eastern Gate;
2. If you hasten off to glory Linger near the Eastern Gate;
3. Keep your lamps all trimmed and burning, For the Bridegroom watch and wait.
4. O, the joy of that glad meeting With the saints who for us wait!

Then be ready, faithful pilgrim, Lest with you it be too late.
For I'm coming in the morning, So you'll not have long to wait.
He'll be with us at the meeting, Just inside the Eastern Gate.
What a blessed, happy meeting, Just inside the Eastern Gate!

I will meet you in the morning, I will meet you in the morning, just inside the Eastern Gate over there; I will meet you in the morning I will meet you in the morning, I will meet you in the morning over there.

This Arrangement © 1981 by JIMMY SWAGGART MINISTRIES, P.O. Box 2550, Baton Rouge, LA 70821

When We All Get To Heaven

ELIZA E. HEWITT, 1851-1920
EMILY D. WILSON, 1865-1942

1. Sing the won-drous love of Je-sus; Sing His mer-cy and His grace.
2. While we walk the pil-grim path-way, Clouds will o-ver-spread the sky;
3. Let us then be true and faith-ful, Trust-ing, serv-ing ev-'ry-day.
4. On-ward to the prize be-fore us! Soon His beau-ty we'll be-hold.

In the man-sions, bright and bless-ed, He'll pre-pare for us a place.
But when trav-'ling days are o-ver, Not a shad-ow, not a sigh!
Just one glimpse of Him in glo-ry Will the toils of life re-pay.
Soon the pearl-y gates will o-pen; We shall tread the streets of gold.

REFRAIN

When we all get to heav-en, What a day of re-joic-ing that will be! When we all see Jesus, We'll sing and shout the vic-to-ry.

When we all — What a day of re-joic-ing — When we all — and shout the vic-to-ry.

This Arrangement © 1981 by JIMMY SWAGGART MINISTRIES, P.O. Box 2550, Baton Rouge, LA 70821

Let's Just Praise The Lord

Words by
WILLIAM J. and GLORIA GAITHER

Music by
WILLIAM J. GAITHER

1. We thank You for Your kind-ness, We thank You for Your love, We've been in heav'n-ly pla-ces, felt bless-ings from a-bove; We've been shar-ing all the good things, the fam-'ly can af-ford, Let's just turn our praise t'ward heav-en, and praise the Lord.

2. Just the pre-cious name of Je-sus is worth-y of our praise, Let us bow our knee be-fore Him, our hands to heav-en raise; When He comes in clouds of Glo-ry, with Him to ev-er reign, Let's lift our hap-py voic-es, and praise His dear Name. Let's just

© Copyright 1972 by WILLIAM J. GAITHER (ASCAP).
International Copyright Secured. All Rights Reserved.
Printed by Permission of THE BENSON COMPANY, INC., Nashville.

praise ___ the Lord! ___ Praise ___ the Lord! ___ Let's just
lift our hands to heav-en and praise ___ the Lord; Let's just
praise ___ the Lord, ___ praise ___ the Lord, ___ Let's just
lift our hands t'ward heav-en and praise the Lord. ___

Keep On The Firing Line

J. R. BAXTER Jr.

1. If you're in the bat-tle for the Lord and right, Keep on the fir-ing line, If you win the vic-t'ry, broth-er, you must fight, Keep on the fir-ing line; There are man-y dan-gers which we all must face, If we die still fight-ing it is no dis-grace,

2. God will on-ly use a sol-dier He can trust, Keep on the fir-ing line, If you wear the crown, then bear the cross you must, Life is but to la-bor for the Mas-ter dear, Help to ban-ish dark-ness and to spread good cheer,

3. When we get to heav-en we shall be so glad, We shall praise the Sav-ior for the call we had, my broth-er; 'Twill be joy to see the souls we helped to win, Those we led to Je-sus, from the paths of sin,

© Copyright 1946. © Renewed 1974 by STAMPS-BAXTER MUSIC & PTG. CO.
All Rights Reserved. Used by Permission.

Cow - ards in the ser - vice should not have a place,
We shall be re - ward - ed for our ser - vice here,
Hear their wel - come plau - dit and go march - ing in,

CHORUS

Keep on the fir - ing line. — You must fight and be brave a-
fir - ing line.

gainst all e - vil, Nev - er run, tho' foes com - bine; If you

would fight for God and right, Keep on the fir - ing line. —
fir - ing line.

Wait'll You See My Brand New Home

Words and Music by
RUSTY GOODMAN

1. If you're awed by this world and all its beau-ty, man-y state-ly man-sions dai-ly you may see. But with-out great wealth I know I'll nev-er own one, and you will nei-ther if you're no more rich than me; But if your soul will look be-yond what man is build-ing, you can see what earth-ly mor-tals can-not see, For on the

2. My new home will not be set up on foun-da-tions that are made by man and will some day pass a-way. It won't be built where the storms of life can bat-ter, where the storm clouds of-ten hide the light of day; But the Cor-ner-stone of God is my foun-da-tion, the Root of Da-vid, Christ, the Lord, the com-ing King, What a

© Copyright 1976 by CANAANLAND MUSIC (a div. of WORD INC.)
International Copyright Secured. All Rights Reserved. Used by Permission.

oth-er side of Jor-dan there's con-struc-tion on a man-sion be-ing
wel-come and home-com-ing that a-waits me, and I'm ex-pect-ing an-y

built just for me. And just wait-'ll you see my brand new home.
day to move right in.

CHORUS

Wait-'ll you see its beau-ty rare, there's noth-ing down here that can com-pare;

Just wait-'ll you see my brand new home, My heav-en-ly Fa-ther's build-ing

me, and I'm gon-na oc-cu-py for free, Just wait-'ll you see my brand new home.

He Set Me Free

ALBERT E. BRUMLEY

1. Once like a bird in pris-on I dwelt,— No free-dom from my sor-row I felt, But Je-sus came and lis-tened to me And glo-ry to God, He set me free.
2. Now I am climb-ing high-er each day,— Dark-ness of night has drift-ed a-way; My feet are plant-ed on high-er ground, And glo-ry to God, I'm home-ward bound.
3. Good-by to sin and things that con-found,— Naught of the world shall turn me a-round; Dai-ly I'm work-ing, I'm pray-ing, too, And glo-ry to God, I'm go-ing thru.

CHORUS

He set me free, yes, He set me free, He broke the bonds of pris-on for me;— And I'm glo-ry bound my Je-sus to see, For glo-ry to God, He set me free.

© Copyright 1939 by STAMPS-BAXTER MUSIC & PTG. Co. in "Gospel Tide".
© Renewal 1967. All Rights Reserved. Used by Permission.

When The Saints Go Marching In

TRADITIONAL

1. I'm just a weary pilgrim, trav-'ling thru this world of sin; Gettin' ready for that meeting, When the saints go marching in.
2. Just a few more days to travel, just a few more days to roam; Then I'll enter Heaven's portals, When the saints are gathered home.
3. There's a place that He's prepared us, if we journey to the end; Then a crown of life He'll give us, When the saints go marching in.

CHORUS

O, when the saints, go marching in, O, when the saints go marching in. O, Lord, I want to be in that number When the saints go marching in.

This Arrangement © 1981 by JIMMY SWAGGART MINISTRIES, P.O. Box 2550, Baton Rouge, LA 70821

Redemption Draweth Nigh

Words and Music by
GORDON JENSEN

1. Years of time have come and gone since I first heard it told
How Jesus would come again some day;
If back then it seemed so real, then I just can't help but feel
How much closer His coming is today.

2. Wars and strife on ev-'ry hand, and violence fills the land,
Still some people doubt He'll come again;
But the Word of God is true, He'll redeem His chosen few,
Don't lose hope, soon Christ Jesus will descend.

© Copyright 1970 by GOLDLINE MUSIC, INC. (ASCAP)
329 Rockland Road, Hendersonville, TN. 37075
All Rights Reserved. International Copyright Secured.

CHORUS

Signs of the times are ev-'ry-where.

And there's a brand new feel-ing in the air;

Keep your eyes up-on the east-ern sky,

Lift up your head, re-demp-tion draw-eth nigh.

Ten Thousand Years

Words and Music by
ELMER COLE

Soon I'll come to the end of my jour-ney,
We will just be-gin to sing love's sweet stor-y;

And I'll meet the One who gave His life for me;
It's a song that the an-gels can-not sing:

I will thank Him for the love that He gave me,
"I'm re-deemed by the blood of the Sav-ior"

And ten thou-sand years or more I'll reign with Him.
And ten thou-sand years or more I'll praise His name.

©Copyright 1970 by HEARTWARMING MUSIC CO. (BMI).
International Copyright Secured. All Rights Reserved.
Printed by Permission of THE BENSON COMPANY, INC., Nashville.

CHORUS

Ten thousand years we'll just be started, ten thousand years we've just begun; The battle's over and the vict'ry's been won, ten thousand years and we've just begun.

Heartmender

Words and Music by
AARON WILBURN
and DAVE LEHMAN

1. Right now you feel like you're the only person that ever had a broken heart. Now you're searchin' for new beginnings but you don't know where to start. You put your hope in time as a healer time passes by so slowly. Have you ever tho't of looking to Jesus. You may be surprised

© Copyright 1981 by PRIME TIME MUSIC, a div. of J. AARON BROWN & ASSOC., INC.
825 19th Ave. South, Nashville, TN 37203 U.S.A.
All Rights Reserved. International Copyright Secured.

at what you see _____ He's the heart-mend-er He's the heart-mend-er He's the sun-shine send-er, And tho' you feel like ___ your heart is bro-ken in two, just give Je-sus a chance, let Him prove _____ He's the heart-mend-er _____ He's the heart-mend-er, He's the heart-mend-er. _____

2. I know sometimes love can seem hopeless
   When you feel you've lost everything
   From where you're standing the rainbow is hidden
   And all you can feel is the rain
   Now it's alright to cry for a while
   But don't let sadness bring you down
   Did you know that Jesus may have something for you
   Much better than anything you could have found.

Leaning On The Everlasting Arms

Rev. E. A. HOFFMAN A. J. SHOWALTER

1. What a fel-low-ship, what a joy di-vine, Lean-ing on the ev-er-last-ing arms; What a bless-ed-ness, what a peace is mine, Lean-ing on the ev-er-last-ing arms.
2. O how sweet to walk in the pil-grim way, Lean-ing on the ev-er-last-ing arms; O how bright the path grows from day to day, Lean-ing on the ev-er-last-ing arms.
3. What have I to dread, what have I to fear, Lean-ing on the ev-er-last-ing arms; I have bless-ed peace with my Lord so near, Lean-ing on the ev-er-last-ing arms.

CHORUS

Lean-ing, lean-ing, Lean-ing on Je-sus, lean-ing on Je-sus Safe and se-cure from all al-arms; Lean-ing on the ev-er-last-ing arms.

This Arrangement ©1981 by JIMMY SWAGGART MINISTRIES, P.O. Box 2550, Baton Rouge, LA 70821

He Did It All For Me

Words and Music by
DUANE ALLEN
and SAGER POWELL

1. Once a man, whom we know as the Son of God, Hung up-on a cru-el tree; He suf-fered pain as no mor-tal man, He took my place, He did it all for me. He did it all for me. Each drop of blood, He shed for ev-en me; When the Sav-ior cried, bowed His head and died. Oh, praise the Lord, He did it all for me.

2. When I step just in-side of those gates of pearl. And the Mas-ter's face I see; I'll glad-ly kneel at His nail-scarred feet, Oh, praise the Lord, He did it all for me.

© Copyright 1970 by SILVERLINE MUSIC, INC. (BMI)
329 Rockland Road, Hendersonville, TN 37075
All Rights Reserved. International Copyright Secured.

Learning To Lean

Words and Music by
JOHN STALLINGS

Slowly

CHORUS

I'm learn-ing to lean, learn-ing to lean, Learn-ing to lean on Je - sus; Find-ing more pow-er than I'd ev-er dreamed; I'm learn-ing to lean on Je - sus.

© Copyright 1976 by HEARTWARMING MUSIC CO. (BMI).
International Copyright Secured. All Rights Reserved.
Printed by Permission of THE BENSON COMPANY, INC., Nashville.

VERSES

1. The joy I can't ex-plain fills my soul, Since the day I made Jesus my King; His blessed Holy Spirit is leading my way, He's teaching and I'm learning to lean.

2. Sometimes we can be like the man who said, "My life is full now, I have ev'rything"; But there is a strong Rock in Jesus, my Lord; Thro' my trials I've been learning to lean.

3. Sad, broken-hearted, so often I've knelt, And I've found God's peace so serene; And all that He asks is a child-like trust, And a heart that is learning to lean.

4. There's glorious vict'ry each day now for me, I found His peace so serene; He helps me with each task if only I'll ask; Ev'ry day now I'm learning to lean.

D.S. al Coda

CODA

I'm Jesus.

Keep Walking

JAMES THOMAS TUCK

1. I searched and I searched for the road that leads to glo-ry,
2. I prayed and I prayed for the Lord to give me mer-cy,

I won-dered if I'd ev-er find the way;
I prayed for Him to bright-en up the day;

I sat down to rest, for my feet had grown so wea-ry,
I was so a-fraid, for the road now seemed so lone-ly,

But then I heard a voice with-in me say.

© Copyright 1957 by TENNESSEE MUSIC and PRINTING CO., in "Billows Of Love"
All Rights Reserved. Used by Permission.

CHORUS

You've got to keep on walk-ing, Keep on walk-ing, Walk-ing in the light of the Lord; You'll get to heav-en some-day, bet-ter get in the right way, Walk-ing in the light of the Lord.

The Great Reward

Words and Music by
HAL and RACHEL NEWMAN

1. When the chil-dren of cre-a-tion be-come the le-gal heirs, there'll be peace a-mong the na-tions, pow-er in our prayers, when the will of the peo-ple is the way of the Lord, we will all join to-geth-er and reap the great re-ward.

CHORUS
We will reap the great re-ward, with-out shield,

© Copyright 1981 by PRIME TIME MUSIC, a div. of J. AARON BROWN & ASSOC., INC.
825 19th Ave. South, Nashville, TN 37203 U.S.A.
All Rights Reserved. International Copyright Secured.

— with-out sword,— when we look face to face in-to the eyes— of the Lord that's the day we will reap the great — re-ward.

Additional verses:

2. When He comes again in glory to claim us for His own
   He will tell the greatest story the world has ever known
   When the fountains of His mercy run like rivers to the shore
   We will all join together and reap the great reward.

3. When the day of understanding is dawning on the land
   Every heart will turn to Jesus, it's in the master plan
   There'll be singing on the mountain, we'll be lifting up the Lord
   When Jesus comes again, we will reap the great reward.

Deliverance Will Come

TRADITIONAL

1. I saw a way-worn trav-'ler in tat-tered gar-ments clad; While strug-gling up the moun-tain, it seemed that he was sad. His back was la-den heav-y; his strength was al-most gone; But he shout-ed as he jour-neyed, "De-liv-er-ance will come!"
2. I saw Him in the eve-ning; the sun was bend-ing low, Had o-ver-topped the moun-tain and reached the vale be-low. While ga-zing t'ward that cit-y: his ev-er-last-ing home, He shout-ed loud ho-san-nas, "De-liv-er-ance will come!"
3. He saw the Ho-ly Cit-y, his ev-er-last-ing home; A band of ho-ly an-gels all gath-er-ed 'round God's throne. They bore Him on their pin-ions safe o'er the dash-ing foam; And they shout-ed "Hal-le-lu-jah! De-liv-er-ance will come!"

CHORUS *Chorus may be repeated.*

Then palms of vic-to-ry, Crowns of glo-ry; Palms of vic-to-ry I shall wear!
palms　　　　　　　　　Crowns　　　　　　　Palms

This Arrangement © 1981 by JIMMY SWAGGART MINISTRIES, P.O. Box 2550, Baton Rouge, LA 70821

He's Got The Whole World In His Hands

TRADITIONAL SPIRITUAL

1. He's got the whole wide world in His hands,
2. He's got the wind and the rain in His hands,
3. He's got that tiny little baby in His hands,
4. He's got you and me, brother, in His hands,
5. He's got ev-'ry-bod-y in His hands,

He's got the big round world in His hands,
He's got the sun and the moon in His hands,
He's got that help-less lit-tle ba-by in His hands,
He's got you and me, sis-ter, in His hands,
He's got ev-'ry-bod-y in His hands,

He's got the whole wide world in His hands
He's got the wind and the rain in His hands
He's got that ti-ny lit-tle ba-by in His hands
He's got you and me, broth-er, in His hands
He's got ev-'ry-bod-y in His hands

He's got the whole world in His hands.
He's got the whole world in His hands.
He's got the whole world in His hands.
He's got the whole world in His hands.
He's got the whole world in His hands.

This Arrangement © 1981 by JIMMY SWAGGART MINISTRIES, P.O. Box 2550, Baton Rouge, LA 70821

Turn Your Radio On

Words and Music by ALBERT E. BRUMLEY

1. Come and lis-ten in to a ra-di-o sta-tion where the might-y hosts of Heav-en sing, Turn your ra-di-o on, turn your ra-di-o on; If you want to hear the songs of Zi-on com-ing from the land of end-less spring,

2. Broth-er lis-ten in to the glo-ry land cho-rus, lis-ten to the glad ho-san-nas roll, Turn your ra-di-o on, turn your ra-di-o on; Get a lit-tle taste of joy a-wait-ing, get a lit-tle Heav-en in your soul,

3. Lis-ten to the songs of the fa-thers and moth-ers and the man-y friends gone on be-fore, Turn your ra-di-o on, turn your ra-di-o on; Some e-ter-nal morn-ing we shall meet them o-ver on the hal-le-lu-jah shore,

© Copyright 1938 by STAMPS-BAXTER MUSIC & PTG. CO. in "Guiding Star".
© Renewal 1966. All Rights Reserved. Used by Permission.

Get in touch with God, turn your ra-di-o on.
Get in touch with God, turn your ra-di-o on.

CHORUS

Turn your ra-di-o on,
Turn your ra-di-o on and lis-ten to the mu-sic in the air,

Turn your ra-di-o on, Heav-en's glo-ry share;
Turn your ra-di-o on, Heav-en's glo-ry share;

Turn the lights down low
Turn the lights down low And lis-ten to the Mas-ter's ra-di-o,

Get in touch with God, turn your ra-di-o on.
Get in touch with God,

Just Any Day Now

Words and Music by
EDDIE CROOK
and AARON WILBURN

1. Each time I stop and take the time to look a-round me,
2. Oh, there's a long-ing in my heart for His ap-pear-ing,

I see the signs of His ap-pear-ing ev-'ry-where;
I'll glad-ly leave be-hind these tri-als here be-low;

The things He said would come to pass are now be-fore us,
For this jour-ney has been long and I'm so wea-ry,

— And I feel a strange ex-cite-ment in the air.
But, Lord, some-how I feel I'm so much clos-er home.

© Copyright 1975 by JOURNEY MUSIC, CO. Assigned to CANAANLAND MUSIC (a div. of WORD, INC.)
All Rights Reserved. International Copyright Secured. Used by Permission.

CHORUS

Just an-y day now our Lord is com-ing,
He'll be re-turn-ing for you and me;
For I've been watch-ing, and I've been wait-ing,
Just an-y day now His face I'll see.

I See Jesus

Words and Music by
CHARLES B. WYCUFF

1. Once a man named Ste-phen, preached a-bout the Lord,
2. As the stones fell on him, beat-ing out his life,
3. Thro' the gates of glo-ry, down the streets of gold,

Folks were saved and folks were healed, As they heard his word;
Ste-phen knew he'd soon be thro', with all toil and strife;
Marched a he-ro of the Lord, In-to heav-en's fold;

Sa-tan did not like it, soon he had his crowd,
So much did like the Mas-ter, with a heart so true,
When he met the Sav-ior, at the great white throne,

And as he was tried they heard Ste-phen cry a-loud.
He prayed "Lord, for-give, for they know not what they do."
I be-lieve He smiled and said, "Ste-phen, wel-come home."

©Copyright 1957 by TENNESSEE MUSIC and PRINTING Co., in "Billows Of Love".
All Rights Reserved. Used by Permission.

CHORUS

"I see Jesus, standing at the Father's right hand,

I see Jesus, yonder in the promised land;

Work is over, Now I'm coming to Thee,

I see Jesus, standing waiting for me."

Victory In Jesus

E. M. BARTLETT

1. I heard an old, old story, how a Savior came from glory,
   How He gave His life on Calvary to save a wretch like me;
   I heard about His groaning, of His precious blood's atoning,
   Then I repented of my sins and won the victory.

2. I heard about His healing, of His cleansing pow'r revealing,
   How He made the lame to walk again and caused the blind to see;
   And then I cried, "Dear Jesus, come and heal my broken spirit,"
   And somehow Jesus came and bro't to me the victory.

3. I heard about a mansion He has built for me in glory,
   And I heard about the streets of gold beyond the crystal sea;
   About the angels singing, and the old redemption story.
   And some sweet day I'll sing up there the song of victory.

© Copyright 1939 by ALBERT E. BRUMLEY & SONS
© Copyright 1967 by ALBERT E. BRUMLEY & SONS, Renewal
All Rights Reserved.

CHORUS

O victory in Jesus, my Savior, forever He sought me and bought me with His redeeming blood. He loved me ere I knew Him, and all my love is due Him. He plunged me to victory beneath the cleansing flood.

The Lighthouse

Words and Music by RONNIE HINSON

1. There's a light-house on the hill-side that o-ver-looks life's sea, When I'm tossed it sends out a light, that I might see; "And the light that shines in darkness, now will safe-ly lead us o'er, If it was-n't for the light-house, my ship would be no more.

2. Ev-'ry-bod-y that lives a-bout us says, "Tear that light-house down; The big ships don't sail this way an-y-more, there's no use of it stand-ing 'round; Then my mind goes back to that storm-y night, when just in time I saw the light, Yes, the light from that old light-house, that stands up there on the hill.

© Copyright 1971 by CANAANLAND MUSIC (a div. of WORD, INC.)
International Copyright Secured. All Rights Reserved. Used by Permission.

CHORUS

And I thank God for the light-house, I owe my life to Him; For Jesus is the light-house, and from the rocks of sin He has shone a light around me that I could clearly see; If it wasn't for the light-house, tell me, where would this ship be?

I've Been To Calvary

Words and Music by
WILLIAM J. GAITHER

1. I've never traveled far around the world, I've never seen the many thrills and sights unfurled; But I have taken the journey of journeys for me, Up Calv'ry's Mountain, there my Savior to see.

2. I walked the Calv'ry road, where Jesus trod, I saw Him hanging there, The Son of God; With tear-stained eyes I knelt and prayed, Jesus, hear my plea, Oh, praise the Lord, I'm glad I've been to Calvary.

© Copyright 1960 by BEN SPEER MUSIC.
All Rights Reserved and Controlled by BEN SPEER MUSIC, Box 40201, Nashville, 37204
International Copyright Secured.   Used by Permission.

CHORUS

I've been to Calvary, I can say I've seen the Lord, I've been to Calvary, Through the witness of His Word, Each day at Calvary, What a thrill of love Divine, Just to know that this Savior is mine.

Just to think, Just to feel, Just to know that this Savior is mine.

Will The Circle Be Unbroken

A. P. CARTER

1. I was stand-ing by my win-dow, on one cold and cloud-y day.
2. Oh, I told the un-der-tak-er, "Un-der-tak-er please drive slow.
3. I will fol-low close be-hind her, try to hold up and be brave.

When I saw the hearse come roll-ing, For to take my Moth-er a-way.
For this bod-y you are haul-ing, Lord, I hate to see her go".
But I could not hide my sor-row, When they laid her in her grave.

Will the cir-cle be un-bro-ken, by and by, Lord, by and by?

There's a bet-ter home a-wait-ing, in the sky, in the sky.

© Copyright 1907, CHARLES M. ALEXANDER. ©Renewed 1935, THE RODEHEAVER CO.
(a div. of WORD, INC.)   Used by Permission.

Have Faith In God

1. Have faith in God when your path-way is lone-ly, He sees and knows all the way you have trod; Nev-er a-lone are the least of His chil-dren; Have faith in God, have faith in God.

2. Have faith in God when your pray'rs are un-an-swered, Your ear-nest plea He will nev-er for-get; Wait on the Lord, trust His Word and be pa-tient, Have faith in God, He'll an-swer yet.

3. Have faith in God in your pain and your sor-row, His heart is touched with your grief and des-pair; Cast all your cares and your bur-dens up-on Him, And leave them there, oh, leave them there.

4. Have faith in God tho' all else fail a-bout you; Have faith in God, He pro-vides for His own; He can-not fail and tho' all king-doms shall per-ish, He rules, He reigns up-on His throne.

Have faith in God, He's on His throne; Have faith in God, He watch-es o'er His own; He can-not fail, He must pre-vail; Have faith in God, have faith in God.

©Copyright 1934. Renewal 1962 BROADMAN PRESS.
All Rights Reserved. Used by Permission.

I'd Rather Be An Old Time Christian

ALBERT E. BRUMLEY

1. In this world I've tried most ev-'ry-thing, And I'm hap-py now to say, There is noth-ing like re-lig-ion In the good old fash-ioned way; I am walk-ing in the old-time way, And I want the world to know That I'd rath-er be an old-time

2. There are man-y things I'd like to be As my jour-ney I pur-sue, I have longed to be a lead-er Like a mor-tal man would do; I would like to be a mil-lion-aire, With a mil-lion to be-stow, But I'd rath-er be an old-time

3. All the world is bright since I got right, Now I sing and pray and shout, All my bur-dens have been lift-ed Since the Sav-ior bro't me out; I will tell the world both far and near As I trav-el here be-low, That I'd rath-er be an old-time

© Copyright 1934 by ALBERT E. BRUMLEY & SONS.
© Copyright 1962 by ALBERT E. BRUMLEY & SONS, Renewal.
All Rights Reserved.

Chris-tian, (Lord,) Than an-y-thing I know. I'd rath-er be an old-time

CHORUS

Chris-tian, (Lord,) Than an-y-thing I know, There's noth-ing like an old-time

Chris-tian With a Chris-tian love to show; I'm walk-ing in the grand old

high-way, And I'm tell-ing ev-'ry-where I go, That I'd

rath-er be an old-time Chris-tian Than an-y-thing I know. (Lord,)

He Was There All The Time

Words and Music by
GARY S. PAXTON

1. Time af-ter time I went search-in' for peace in some void;____ I was
2. Nev-er a-gain will I look for a fake rain-bow's end;____ Now that

try-ing to blame all my ills on this world I was in.
I have the an-swer, my life is just start-ing to rhyme.

Sur-face re-la-tion-ships used me 'til I was done in;____ And
Shar-ing each new day with Him is a cup of fresh life;____ —

all the while Some-one was beg-ging to free me from sin.
Oh, what I missed, He's been wait-ing right there all the time.

© Copyright 1975 by NEW PAX MUSIC PRESS (ASCAP).
International Copyright Secured. All Rights Reserved.
Printed by Permission of THE BENSON COMPANY, INC., Nashville.

CHORUS

He was there all the time, He was there all the time; Waiting patiently in line, He was there all the time.

time.

Go Tell It On The Mountain

TRADITIONAL SPIRITUAL

CHORUS

Go tell it on the moun-tain, O-ver the hills and ev-'ry-where;
Go tell it on the moun-tain, That Je-sus Christ is born!

1. When I was a seek-er, I sought both night and day; I asked the Lord to help me, and He showed me the way.
2. He made me a watch-man up-on the cit-y wall; And tho I am a Chris-tian, I am the least of all.

This Arrangement © 1981 by JIMMY SWAGGART MINISTRIES, P.O. Box 2550, Baton Rouge, LA 70821

I Will Serve Thee

WILLIAM J. and GLORIA GAITHER
WILLIAM J. GAITHER

I will serve Thee because I love Thee, You have given life to me; I was nothing before You found me, You have given life to me; Heart-aches, broken pieces, Ruined lives are why You died on Cal-v'ry, Your touch was what I longed for, You have given life to me.

© Copyright 1969 by WILLIAM J. GAITHER (ASCAP).
All Rights Reserved. International Copyright Secured.
Printed by Permission of THE BENSON COMPANY, INC., Nashville.

Reach Out To Jesus

Words and Music by
RALPH CARMICHAEL

1. Is your bur-den heav-y as you bear it all a-lone?
2. Is the life you're liv-ing filled with sor-row and des-pair?

Does the road you trav-el har-bor dan-ger yet un-known?
Does the fu-ture press you with its wor-ry and its care?

Are you grow-ing wear-y in the strug-gle of it all?
Are you tired and friend-less, Have you al-most lost your way?

Je-sus will help you when on His name you call.
Je-sus will help you, just come to Him to-day.

© Copyright 1968 by LEXICON MUSIC, INC. ASCAP
All Rights Reserved. International Copyright Secured. Used by Permission.

He is al-ways there hear-ing ev-'ry prayer, faith-ful and true,

Walk-ing by our side, in His love we hide all the day through.

When you get dis-cour-aged just re-mem-ber what to do

Reach out to Je-sus, He's reach-ing out to you. you.

Goodbye World, Goodbye

Words and Music by
MOSIE LISTER

I've told all my trou-bles good-by,— Good-by to each tear and each sigh;— This
won't have the blues an-y-more— when I step a-cross to that shore.— And

world where I roam can-not be my home I'm bound for a land in the sky.— I
I'll nev-er pine for I'll leave be-hind my heart-aches and tears ev-er-more,— A

walk and I talk with my Lord,— I feast ev-'ry-day on His word.—
day may be two, then good-by— To-mor-row I'll rise up and fly.—

Heav-en is near, and I can't stay here, Good-by world, good-by.—

© Copyright 1955 by LILLENAS PUBLISHING CO.
All Rights Reserved. Used by Permission.

REFRAIN

Now don't you weep for me when I'm gone 'cause I won't have to leave here alone; And when I hear the last trumpet sound, My feet won't stay on the ground. Gonna rise with a shout; Gonna fly, gonna ride with my Lord thru the sky. Heaven is near, and I can't stay here, Good-by world, good-by. I by.

He Lives

A. H. ACKLEY

I serve a ris-en Sav-ior, He's in the world to-day;_ I
In all the world a-round me I see His lov-ing care,_ And
Re-joice, re-joice O Chris-tian, lift up your voice and sing_ E-

know that He is liv-ing, what-ev-er men may say;_ I
tho' my heart grows wea-ry I nev-er will des-pair;_ I
ter-nal hal-le-lu-jahs to Je-sus Christ the King!_ The

see His hand of mer-cy, I hear His voice of
know that He is lead-ing, thro' all the storm-y
Hope of all who seek Him, the Help of all who

cheer,_ And just the time I need Him_ He's al-ways near._
blast,_ The day of His ap-pear-ing_ will come at last._
find,_ None oth-er is so lov-ing,_ so good and kind._

© Copyright 1933 by HOMER A. RODEHEAVER.©Renewed 1961,
THE RODEHEAVER CO. (a div. of WORD, INC.)
All Rights Reserved. International Copyright Secured. Used by Permission.

REFRAIN

He lives, He lives, Christ Jesus lives today! He walks with me and talks with me along life's narrow way. He lives, He lives, salvation to impart! You ask me how I know He lives? He lives within my heart.

That's The Man I'm Looking For

Words and Music by DON LEE

1. If you see a Man in san-dals, please send Him down my way;
2. If you see a Man that shines with a love glow on His face;

It might be my Mas-ter— He's com-ing back— some day;
Turn Him down my street— So He can find— my place;

If you see a Man in white that's like no one you've seen be-fore,
And— if His hands are scarred— please don't shut the door,

— Won't you let me know, That's the Man I'm look-ing for.
Just send Him on to me, That's the Man I'm look-ing for.

© Copyright 1972 by SONG OF CASH, INC.
P.O. Box 508, Hendersonville, Tennessee 37075
All Rights Reserved. Used by Permission.

CHORUS

And if you can remember, ask Him what's His name;
And if He tells you Jesus, say, "We're so glad You came."
Tell Him you know someone that still calls Him Lord,
Then send Him on to me, that's the Man I'm looking for.

What Sins Are You Talking About

Words and Music by
HAROLD LANE
and BEN L. SPEER

1. I remember the days when I was bent low With the burden of sin and strife, Then Jesus came in and rescued me, and He gave me a brand new life; And now as I thank Him day after day for washing my sins away, It
2. When my flesh becomes weak it's then I can speak To the Savior who's with me each day, "Oh, Father, forgive me, hear my plea," and He washes my sin away; Each time that I bow to give Him thanks for removing my guilt and shame, He

© Copyright 1978 by BEN SPEER MUSIC.
All Rights Reserved and Controlled by BEN SPEER MUSIC, Box 40201, Nashville, 37204
International Copyright Secured.   Used by Permission.

seems I can al-most hear the voice of the Bless-ed Sav-ior say.
can-not re-call what I'm talk-in' a-bout, for His answer is al-ways the same.

CHORUS

"What sins are you talk-in' a-bout, I don't re-mem-ber them an-y-more; From the Book of Life they've all been torn out, I don't re-mem-ber them an-y-more."

Jesus Is Coming Soon

Words and Music by
R. E. WINSETT

1. Trou-ble-some times are here, fill-ing men's hearts with fear, Free-dom we all hold dear now is at stake; Hum-bling your heart to God, saves from the chast-'ning rod, Seek the way pil-grims trod, Chris-tians, a - wake.
2. Love of so man-y cold, los-ing their home of gold, This in God's Word is told, e-vils a-bound; When these signs come to pass, near-ing the end at last, It will come ver-y fast, trum-pets will sound.
3. Trou-bles will soon be o'er, hap-py for-ev-er-more, When we meet on that shore, free from all care; Ris-ing up in the sky, tell-ing this world good-bye, Home-ward we then will fly, glo-ry to share.

© Copyright 1942 in "Joys Supernal". Renewed 1969.
Arr. © Copyright 1968, R.E. WINSETT MUSIC CO., ELLIS J. CRUM,
PUBLISHER, Kendallville, Indiana 46755.   Used by Permission.

CHORUS

Je-sus is com-ing soon, morn-ing or night or noon, Man-y will meet their doom, Trum-pets will sound; All of the dead shall rise, Right-eous meet in the skies, Go-ing where no one dies, Heav-en-ward bound. bound.

Com-ing soon, night or noon, Man-y will meet their doom, Trum-pets will sure-ly sound; Dead shall rise, in the skies, Go-ing where no one dies,

Daddy Sang Bass

**Words and Music by
CARL PERKINS**

1. I remember when I was a lad, times were hard and things were bad;
2. I remember after work, mama would call in all of us;

But there's a silver lining behind ev'ry cloud. ___ Just poor
You could hear us singin' for a country mile. ___ Now, little

people, that's all we were, try'n' to make a livin' out of black land dirt;
brother has done gone on, ___ but I'll rejoin him in a song;

We'd get together in a fam'ly circle singin' loud. ___
We'll be together again up yonder in a little while. ___

CHORUS
Daddy sang bass, mama sang tenor, me and little brother would join right in there;

© Copyright 1968 CEDARWOOD PUBLISHING CO., INC. & HOUSE OF CASH
All Rights Reserved. International Copyright Secured.

Sing-in' seems to help a trou-bled soul. One of these days, and it won't be long, I'll re-join them in a song; I'm gon-na join the fam-'ly cir-cle at the throne. No, the cir-cle won't be bro-ken Bye and bye, Lord, bye and bye. Dad-dy sang bass, ma-ma sang ten-or, me and lit-tle broth-er would join right in there, in the sky, Lord, in the sky.

John The Revelator

Words and Music by
RUSTY GOODMAN

1. Up-on the Isle of Pat-mos a man was cast one day,
2. While in the Spir-it pray-ing, John turned a-round to see,

As he was left a-lone to die,— he be-gan to pray;
— If the voice— he had heard was what it seemed to be;

The Ho-ly Ghost fell on him, the Spir-it, it came down,
— Just like man-y wat-ers, a great— trum-pet sound,

He be-gan to write a-bout the things he saw, the rev-e-la-tor's name was John.
He— said, "I am— the First and Last," the rev-e-la-tor wrote it down.

© Copyright 1975 by JOURNEY MUSIC CO. (a div. of WORD, INC.)
All Rights Reserved. International Copyright Secured. Used by Permission.

CHORUS

John, the rev-e-la-tor saw Je-ru-sa-lem a-com-ing down,
Talk-ing 'bout John, _____

John, the rev-e-la-tor, and when he looked a-round;
Yes, it was John, _____

He saw feet like brass, eyes like fire, heard a great voice say-ing, "Come up high-er!"

John, the rev-e-la-tor, wrote a-bout the cit-y of God.

Come And Dine

Words and Music by
C.B. WIDMEYER

1. Jesus has a table spread Where the saints of God are fed.
2. The disciples came to land, Thus obeying Christ's command,
3. Soon the Lamb will take His bride To be ever at His side.

He invites His chosen people, "Come and dine." With His manna He doth
For the Master called to them, "Oh, come and dine." There they found their hearts' de-
All the host of heaven will assembled be. Oh, 'twill be a glorious

feed And supplies our ev'ry need. Oh, 'tis sweet to sup with Jesus all the time!
sire, Bread and fish upon the fire. Thus He satisfies the hungry ev'ry time.
sight, All the saints in spotless white; And with Jesus they will feast eternally.

CHORUS

"Come and dine," the Master calleth; "Come and dine (Oh, come and dine)." You may feast at

© Copyright 1914 by JOHN T. BENSON, Jr. Renewed 1942. Copyright extended.
All Rights Reserved. International Copyright Secured. Used by Permission.

Je-sus' ta-ble all the time. (Oh, come and dine!) He who fed the mul-ti-tude,
Turned the wat-er in-to wine, To the hun-gry call-eth now, "Come and dine."

Amazing Grace

JOHN NEWTON, 1725 - 1807
Early American Melody

1. A-maz-ing grace! how sweet the sound! That saved a wretch like me!
2. 'Twas grace that taught my heart to fear, And grace my fears re-lieved.
3. Thro' man-y dan-gers, toils, and snares I have al-read-y come.
4. When we've been there ten thou-sand years, Bright, shin-ing as the sun,

I once was lost, but now am found; Was blind, but now I see.
How pre-cious did that grace ap-pear The hour I first be-lieved!
'Tis grace hath bro't me safe thus far, And grace will lead me home.
We've no less days to sing God's praise Than when we first be-gun.

This Arrangement © 1981 by JIMMY SWAGGART MINISTRIES, P.O. Box 2550, Baton Rouge, LA 70821.

We'll Soon Be Done With Troubles And Trials

Words and Music by
CLEAVANT DERRICKS

1. Some of these days I'm going home where no sorrows ever come,
2. Kindred and friends now wait for me, soon their faces I shall see,
3. I shall behold His blessed face, I shall feel His matchless grace,

We'll soon be done with troubles and trials;
We'll soon be done troubles and trials;

Safe from heart-aches, pain and care, we shall all that glory share,
'Tis a home of life so fair and we'll all be gathered there,
O what peace and joy sublime in that home of love divine.

Sit down beside my Jesus, sit down and
And I'm gonna
Lord, I'm gonna

© Copyright 1934 by STAMPS-BAXTER MUSIC & PTG. CO. in "Pearls of Paradise"
© Renewal 1962 by STAMPS-BAXTER MUSIC & PTG. CO.
All Rights Reserved. Used by Permission.

rest a lit-tle while. We'll soon be done with trou-bles and
We'll soon be done,

tri - als, Yes, in that home on the oth-er
trou-bles and tri - als in that home,

side, Shake glad hands with the eld - ers,
on the oth - er side, And I'm a gon-na

Lord, and tell my kin - dred good morn - ing, Then I'm gon-na

D.S. al Fine

Farther Along

Rev. W. B. STEVENS

1. Tempt-ed and tried we're oft made to won-der Why it should be thus all the day long. While there are oth-ers liv-ing a-bout us, Nev-er mo-lest-ed tho' in the wrong.
2. When death has come and ta-ken our loved ones, It leaves our home so lone-ly and drear; Then do we won-der why oth-ers pros-per, Liv-ing so wick-ed year af-ter year.
3. "Faith-ful till death" said our lov-ing Mas-ter, A few more days to la-bor and wait; Toils of the road will then seem as noth-ing, As we sweep thru the beau-ti-ful gate.
4. When we see Je-sus com-ing in glo-ry, When He comes from His home in the sky; Then we shall meet Him in that bright man-sion, We'll un-der-stand it all by and by.

D.S. We'll un-der-stand it all by and by.

CHORUS

Far-ther a-long we'll know all a-bout it, Far-ther a-long we'll un-der-stand why; Cheer up, my broth-er, live in the sun-shine,

D.S. al Fine

© Copyright 1937 by STAMPS-BAXTER MUSIC & PTG. CO. in "Starlit Crown".
© Renewed 1965. All Rights Reserved. Used by Permission.

Holy Spirit, Thou Art Welcome

Words by DOTTIE RAMBO

Music by DOTTIE RAMBO and DAVE HUNTSINGER

1. Holy Spirit, Thou art welcome in this place; Holy Spirit, Thou art welcome in this place; Omnipotent Father of mercy and grace! Thou art welcome in this place. Lord, in Thy presence there's healing divine; No other power can save, Lord, but Thine; Holy Spirit, Thou art welcome in this place; Thou art welcome in this place.

2. Holy Spirit, Thou art welcome in this place; Holy Spirit, Thou art welcome in this place; Omnipotent Father of mercy and grace! Thou art welcome in this place. Fill all the hungry and empty within; Restore us, oh Father, revive us again; Holy Spirit, Thou art welcome in this place; Thou art welcome in this place.

© Copyright 1977 by HEARTWARMING MUSIC CO.(BMI).
International Copyright Secured. All Rights Secured.
Printed by Permission of THE BENSON COMPANY, INC., Nashville.

Until You've Known The Love Of God

Words and Music by
RUSTY GOODMAN

1. If you could own all the world and its mon-ey,
2. If in your life-time you could meet ev-'ry-bod-y,

Build cas-tles tall e-nough to reach the sky a-bove;
And you could call ev-er-y name from here to yon;

If you could know ev-er-y-thing there was to know a-bout life's game,
But if you've not come face to face with Je-sus and His sav-ing grace,

Yet you've known noth-ing un-til you've known God and His love.
Then you've known no one un-til you've known God and His love.

© Copyright 1975 by JOURNEY MUSIC CO. Assigned to CANAANLAND MUSIC
(a div. of WORD, INC.) All Rights Reserved. International Copyright Secured. Used by Permission.

CHORUS

Until you've known the loving hand that reaches down to a fallen man, And lifts him up from out of sin where he has trod; Until you've known just how it feels to know that God is really real, Then you've known nothing until you've known the love of God.

Just A Little Talk With Jesus

Words and Music by
CLEAVANT DERRICKS

1. I once was lost in sin but Jesus took me in, And then a little light from heaven filled my soul; It bathed my heart in love and wrote my name above, And just a little talk with Jesus made me whole.

2. Sometimes my path seems drear, without a ray of cheer, And then a cloud of doubt may hide the light of day; The mists of sin may rise and hide the starry skies, But just a little talk with Jesus clears the way.

3. I may have doubts and fears, my eyes be filled with tears, But Jesus is a friend who watches day and night; I go to Him in pray'r, He knows my ev'ry care, And just a little talk with Jesus makes it right.

© Copyright 1937 by THE STAMPS-BAXTER MUSIC CO. in "Harbor Bells No. 6".
© Renewed 1965. All Rights Reserved. Used by Permission.

Have a lit-tle talk with Je-sus, tell Him all a-bout our trou-bles,
Now let us let us He will

Hear our faint-est cry, an-swer by and by;
and He will Now when you

Feel a lit-tle pray'r wheel turn-ing, know a lit-tle fire is burn-ing,
and you You will

Find a lit-tle talk with Je-sus makes it right.
It makes it right.

Looking For A City

W. OLIVER COOPER
MARVIN P. DALTON

1. Here a-mong the shad-ows (liv-ing) in a lone-ly land, With stran-gers we're a band of pil-grims on the move;___ Thru dan-gers bur-dened down with sor-rows, And we're shunned on ev-'ry hand, But we are look-ing for a cit-y built a-bove.
2. Here in dis-ap-point-ment (oft-en) we so sad-ly roam, And earth-ly friends no long-er speak one word of love;___ But tru-ly we have found con-tent-ment, Je-sus prom-ised us a Home, So we are look-ing for a cit-y built a-bove.
3. In this land of dan-gers (we are) go-ing here and there, We're sim-ply trust-ing in the bless-ed Sav-ior's love;___ And mer-cy tho' we may be strang-ers, Liv-ing in this world of care, We're al-ways look-ing for a cit-y built a-bove.

a-bove. O yes we're look-ing here and there Look-ing for a cit-y___ Where___ we'll nev-er

Look-ing for a cit-y, Yon-der where we'll nev-er die,

© Copyright 1943 by HARTFORD MUSIC COMPANY.
© Copyright 1971 by ALBERT E. BRUMLEY & SONS and HARTFORD MUSIC COMPANY.
Renewal.   All Rights Reserved.

Bb
die,_____ There_____ the saint-ed mil-lions,_____
nev-er die, no nev-er, And up there with all the saints, yes, with all the mil-lions,

C **F**
Nev - er say good-bye,_____ say good-bye, no nev-er, Yes, and
We will nev-er say good-bye,

Bb **Eb**
There_____ we'll meet our Sav - ior,_____ And_____
When we gath-er there, We'll meet Christ our Sav-ior, Glo-ry, and we know we'll

Bb **Eb**
our loved ones too,_____ Come_____ O ho-ly
meet friends and all our loved ones, Now we pray Thee quick-ly come,

Bb **C** **F7** **Bb** **Eb7** **Bb**
Spir - it,_____ All_____ our hopes re-new._____
Pray Thee come, O spir-it, Come, O come! On Thee we call, All our hopes re-new.

Sweet, Sweet Spirit

DORIS AKERS

1. There's a sweet, sweet, Spir-it in this place,— And I know that it's the Spir-it of the Lord;— There are sweet ex-pres-sions on each face,— And I know they feel the pres-ence of the Lord.—

2. There are bless-ings you can-not re-ceive— 'Til you know Him in His full-ness and be-lieve;— You're the one to pro-fit when you say,— "I am going to walk with Je-sus all the way."—

3. If you say He saved you from your sin, Now you're weak, you're bound and can-not en-ter in;— You can make it right if you will yield,— You'll en-joy the Ho-ly Spir-it that we feel.—

CHORUS

Sweet Ho-ly Spir-it, Sweet hea-ven-ly Dove, Stay right here with us, Fill-ing us with Your love. And for these bless-ings We lift our hearts in praise;— With-out a doubt we'll know that we have been re-vived, When we shall leave this place.—

© Copyright 1962 by MANNA MUSIC, INC., 2111 Kenmere Ave., Burbank, CA. 91504
All Rights Reserved. International Copyright Secured. Used by Permission.

Oh Come, Angel Band

Words by J. HASCALL
Music by WM. B. BRADBURY

1. My latest sun is sinking fast, My race is nearly run;
   My strongest trials now are past, My triumph is begun.
2. I know I'm nearing the holy ranks Of friends and kindred dear,
   For I brush the dews on Jordan's banks, The crossing must be near.
3. I've almost gained my heavenly home, My spirit loudly sings;
   Thy holy ones, behold, they come! I hear the noise of wings.
4. O bear my longing heart to Him, Who bled and died for me;
   Whose blood now cleanses from all sin, And gives me victory.

CHORUS

O come, angel band, Come and around me stand; O bear me away on your snowy wings To my immortal home; O bear me away on your snowy wings To my immortal home.

This Arrangement © 1981 by JIMMY SWAGGART MINISTRIES P.O. Box 2550, Baton Rouge, LA 70821

I'll Meet You In The Morning

Words and Music by
ALBERT E. BRUMLEY

1. I will meet you in the morn-ing by the bright riv-er-side,
2. I will meet you in the morn-ing in the sweet by and by,
3. I will meet you in the morn-ing at the end of the way,

When all sor-row has drift-ed a-way;— I'll be stand-ing at the
And ex-change the old Cross for a crown;— There will be no dis-ap-
On the streets of that Cit-y of Gold;— Where we all can be to-

por-tals when the gates o-pen wide, At the close of life's long, drear-y day.—
point-ments and no-bod-y shall die, In that land e'er the sun go-eth down.—
geth-er and be hap-py for aye, While the years and the a-ges shall roll.—

I'll meet you in the morn-ing.
meet you in the morn-ing, meet you in the morn-ing,

with a "How do you do" And we'll
"How do you do" "How do you do"

© Copyright 1936 by ALBERT E. BRUMLEY & SONS.
© Copyright 1964 by ALBERT E. BRUMLEY & SONS, Renewal. All Rights Reserved.

sit down _____ by the riv - er _____ and with
sit down by the riv - er, sit down by the riv - er,

Cm　　　F7　　Bb　F　Bb　　Eb
rap - ture auld ac - quaint - ance re - new. _____ You'll know _____
rap - ture, our auld ac - quaint - ance re - new, know me in the morn -

Ab
me in the morn - ing, _____ by the smiles _____ that I
ing, know me in the morn - ing, smiles that I wear,

Eb7
wear, _____ when I meet you _____ in the morn - ing, _____
smiles that I wear, meet you in the morn - ing, meet you in the morn - ing,

Bb　　　Eb　Ab　Eb
in the cit - y that is built four - square.
cit - y, cit - y built, that cit - y built four - square.

Jesus Will Outshine Them All

**Words and Music by
GORDON JENSEN**

REFRAIN

Man - sions will glis - ten on the Hills ___ of Glo - ry,
Hap - py re - un - ions on streets of gold, An - gel choirs
Ah ___
sing - ing glad prais - es for - ev - er, ___ But Je - sus will
out - shine ___ them all! ___

1. Oh, ___ what glo - ry ___ a -
2. The spark - ling riv - er ___ is

© Copyright 1972 by JENSEN MUSIC (ASCAP).
International Copyright Secured. All Rights Reserved.
Printed by Permission of THE BENSON COMPANY, INC., Nashville.

waits me — in Heav-en's — bright cit-y, — When I
flow-ing, — Hap-py fac-es — all glow-ing, — Land of

get there — such sights I'll be-hold! — A mil-lion
splen-dor — where night nev-er falls, — The gold-en

scenes of rare beau-ty will de-mand that I view — them, — Still
glass gives re-flec-tion to that cit-y's per-fec-tion — Still

Je-sus will out-shine — them all!
Je-sus will out-shine — them

[1.] all!

[2.] all! *D.S. al Coda*

CODA
out-shine them all!

This Could Be The Dawning Of That Day

Words by
WILLIAM J. and GLORIA GAITHER

Music by
WILLIAM J. GAITHER

1. A pa-rade be-gan at Cal-v'ry, The saints of all the a-ges fill its ranks; O'er the sands of time they're march-ing to their King's great cor-o-na-tion, And this could be the dawn-ing of that day!

2. Noth-ing here holds their al-le-giance, They're not bound by shack-les forged of earth-ly gold; Since that day they knelt at Cal-v'ry, they've been pil-grims e-ver wan-d'ring, Just look-ing for a place to rest their souls.

3. All the saints are get-ting rest-less, Oh, what glo-rious ex-pec-ta-tion fills each face! Dreams and hopes of all the a-ges are a-wait-ing His re-turn-ing, And this could be the dawn-ing of that day!

© Copyright 1971 by WILLIAM J. GAITHER (ASCAP).
International Copyright Secured. All Rights Reserved.
Printed by Permission of THE BENSON COMPANY, INC., Nashville.

CHORUS

Oh, this could be the dawning of that grand and glorious day, When the face of Jesus we behold! Dreams and hopes of all the ages are awaiting His returning, And this could be the dawning of that day! day!

When God Dips His Love In My Heart

Words and Music by CLEAVANT DERRICKS

1. When God dips His pen of love in my heart And writes my soul a message He wants me to know, His Spir-it, all di-vine, fills this sin-ful soul of mine,
2. Some-times tho' the way is drear-y, dark and cold, And some un-bur-dened sor-row keeps me from the goal, I go to God in prayer, I can al-ways find Him there,
3. He walked ev-'ry step up Cal-v'ry's rug-ged way To give His life com-plete-ly, and bring a bet-ter day; My life was steeped in sin, but in love He took me in,

When God dips His love in my heart.
Hal-le-lu-jah! To whis-per sweet peace to my soul.
His blood washed a-way ev-'ry stain.

D.S. Hal-le-lu-jah! When God dips His love in my heart.

© Copyright 1944 (Renewal 1971 by TENNESSEE MUSIC and PRINTING CO. in "Songs Forever".
All Rights Reserved. Used by Permission.

CHORUS

Well, I said I wouldn't tell it to a living soul, How He bro't salvation when He made me whole;— But I found I couldn't hide such love as Jesus did impart;—— 'Cause it makes me laugh, and it makes me cry, then it sets my sinful soul on fire,

I've Got Confidence

Words and Music by
ANDRAE CROUCH

1. When trou-ble is in my way, I can't tell my night from day, When I'm tossed from side to side Like a ship on a rag-ing tide; I don't wor-ry, I don't fret, God has nev-er failed me yet, Trou-bles come from time to time

2. Some folks won-der how I smile E-ven tho' I'm goin' thru trials, How can I have a song When ev-'ry-thing is go-in' wrong;

© Copyright 1969 by LEXICON MUSIC, INC. ASCAP
All Rights Reserved. International Copyright Secured. Used by Special Permission.

But that's all right — I'm not the wor-ry-ing kind: 'Cause,

CHORUS
I've got con-fi-dence, God is gon-na see me thru, No mat-ter what the case may be I know He's gon-na fix it for me.

I Should Have Been Crucified

Words and Music by
GORDON JENSEN

I was guilty ___ with
Crown of thorns, ___ with the

noth-ing ___ to say, ___ And they were com-ing to
spear ___ deep in His side, ___ And the pain ___

take me ___ a-way, ___ But then a voice ___ from
should have ___ been mine, ___ The rust-y nails ___

© Copyright 1972 by JENSEN MUSIC (ASCAP).
International Copyright Secured. All Rights Reserved.
Printed by Permission of THE BENSON COMPANY, INC., Nashville.

heav-en ___ was heard ___ that said, ___ "Let him go! ___
were ___ meant for ___ me, (O,) yet Christ took them ___ and

Take Me in-stead!" ___ And I should have been cru-ci-
let me go free! ___

fied! _____ I should have suf-fered and died! ___
Oo _____

I should have hung on the cross in dis-grace, But

Je-sus, God's Son, took my place! ___ place! ___

He Keeps Me Singing

L. B. B.
LUTHER B. BRIDGERS, 1884-1948

1. There's with-in my heart a mel-o-dy, Je-sus whis-pers sweet and low:
2. All my life was wrecked by sin and strife; Dis-cord filled my heart with pain.
3. Feast-ing on the rich-es of His grace, Rest-ing 'neath His shelt-'ring wing,
4. Tho' some-times He leads thro' wa-ters deep, Tri-als fall a-cross the way,
5. Soon He's com-ing back to wel-come me Far be-yond the star-ry sky.

"Fear not, I am with thee; peace, be still," In all of life's ebb and flow.
Je-sus swept a-cross the bro-ken strings, Stirred the slum-b'ring chords a-gain.
Al-ways look-ing on His smil-ing face, That is why I shout and sing.
Tho' some-times the path seems rough and steep, See His foot-prints all the way.
I shall wing my flight to worlds un-known; I shall reign with Him on high.

REFRAIN

Je-sus, Je-sus, Je-sus, Sweet-est name I know,
Fills my ev-'ry long-ing, Keeps me sing-ing as I go.

© Copyright 1910. Renewal 1937 BROADMAN PRESS.
All Rights Reserved. Used by Permission.